Father, I Must Go

Pierce Kelley

iUniverse, Inc.
Bloomington

Father, I Must Go

iUniverse books may be ordered through booksellers or by contacting:

iUniverse
1663 Liberty Drive
Bloomington, IN 47403
www.iuniverse.com
1-800-Authors (1-800-288-4677)

ISBN: 978-1-4502-8073-0 (pbk)
ISBN: 978-1-4502-8074-7 (ebk)

Printed in the United States of America

iUniverse rev. date: 1/12/2011

Other works by Pierce Kelley

Thousand Yard Stare (iUniverse, 2010);
Kennedy Homes: An American Tragedy (iUniverse, 2009);
A Foreseeable Risk (iUniverse, 2009);
Asleep at the Wheel (iUniverse, 2009);
A Tinker's Damn! (iUniverse, 2008);
Bocas del Toro (iUniverse, 2007);
A Plenary Indulgence (iUniverse, 2007);
Pieces to the Puzzle (iUniverse, 2007);
Introducing Children to the Game of Tennis (iUniverse, 2007);
A Very Fine Line (iUniverse, 2006);
Fistfight at the L and M Saloon (iUniverse, 2006;
Civil Litigation: A Case Study (Pearson Publications, 2001;
The Parent's Guide to Coaching Tennis (F &W Publications, 1995);
A Parent's Guide to Coaching Tennis (Betterway Publications, 1991).

Jorge Frias and his father, Romeo Frias Bobadilla

"To Jorge and his parents, and to all
fathers and mothers whose sons and
daughters have left their homes to go
to foreign countries in search of a better life,
as the Irish have done for centuries."

"Give me your tired, your poor, your huddled masses yearning to breathe free. The wretched refuse of your teaming shore. Send these, the homeless, tempest-tossed to me, I lift my lamp beside the golden door!"

Emma Lazarus (1883)

Acknowledgements

I thank those who have supported and encouraged me on this and other projects. I wish to specifically thank Sue Pundt, Matt and David Sky, Paul Christian Sullivan, Dennis Geagan, Doug Easton and Tug Miller, who have read drafts and offered their insights into this and other works.

The cover photograph was taken of Jorge Frias by Alex Blanco. The photograph of Jorge and his father was taken by Alex Zenios. The photograph on the back cover of Chichen-Itza was taken by Jorge.

In the process of writing this book, I conducted research on various issues relating to the Yucatan Peninsula, the Mayan, Toltec and Aztec civilizations, migration of workers from Mexico to the United States and the Mexican society in general. Those books include: *The Mexicans*, by Patrick Oster (Harper & Row, 1989); *Crossing Over* by Ruben Martinez (Henry Holt & Company, 2001); *No One is Illegal* by Justin Akers Chacon and Mike Davis (Haymarket Books, 2006); *Lost Cities of the Maya* by Claude Baudez and Sydney Picasso (Harry N. Abrams, Inc., 1987); *Yucatan and the Maya Civilization* by Mauricio Wiesenthal (Crescent Books, 1978); *Yucatan Before and After the Conquest* by Diego de Landa Calderon (Forgotten Books, 1937); *The Yucatan* by Antoinette May (World Wide Publishing/Tetra, 1993); *Conversations with Moctezuma*, Dick Reavis (William Morrow and Company, Inc., 1990); *Native American History*, Judith Nies (Ballantine Books, 1996); and *The Ancient Maya*, Sylvanus Griswold Morley, (Stanford University Press, as revised in 1956).

Last, but certainly not least, I acknowledge and thank Jorge, whose story inspired me to write this book. He gave me insight into the world of those who come from Mexico and other places to the United States, most of whom come illegally, some without knowing how to speak English, not knowing if they can make it safely across the border or what they will find if they do. The United States of America will soon decide how to deal with Jorge and those like him, who number in excess of ten million at present, as our immigration policies and procedures are in crisis and are matters of great concern and much public debate at this time.

Pierce Kelley

Prelude:
A Friend of the Wind

I am a Mestizo, born in the city of Progreso in the state of Yucatan, Mexico. A Mestizo is one who has the mixed blood of the indigenous people of the Yucatan and the Spanish conquistadores. There were hundreds of tribes of indigenous peoples, erroneously labeled "Indians" because the Spanish thought they were in India, who lived in the land which now encompasses Mexico, Guatemala, Honduras and Belize prior to the arrival of the Spanish in 1511. Few people now exist in Mexico who are not Mestizo.

Most of my ancestors lived in the Yucatan long before they knew that there were "pale" people with beards living in Spain, Portugal, France or England, or that there were people living in India, Asia, Africa or anywhere outside of Mesoamerica. The Mayan civilization is said to have begun with the "pre-Classic" stage, beginning in approximately 1500.B.C. There were people, my people, living here for thousands of years before that, even before the Sumerian civilization came into being. Though the Mayans abandoned their magnificent cities and temples and their civilization disappeared sometime during the tenth century for no known reason, they did not die. They went back to living in the jungles and the mountains. They still exist today and I am one of their descendants.

I may be descended from Gonzalo Guerrero himself. He was the first Mestizo. In 1511, he and twelve of his Spanish mates survived the wreck of their ship off the coast of Jamaica and, after drifting for thirteen days, came ashore somewhere on the eastern coast of the

Yucatan, not far from the city of Tulum, near what is now Playa del Carmen. They were the first of the white men to arrive.

All of Guerrero's mates, except for Geronimo del Aguilar, died soon after being captured. Several were reportedly sacrificed on an altar to a Mayan god, maybe Chac, the god of rain, as the Yucatan peninsula has never had enough water. Gonzalo and Geronimo were, for some unknown reason, spared. Gonzalo assimilated with the Mayans, married, had children and became a leader of warriors, going so far as to lead Mayans in battle against his former countrymen, the Conquistadors, who came several years later to the Yucatan in search of gold and treasures.

I am presently a guide in Cancun and Playa del Carmen. I still call Progreso home. My family has lived there for a century. I now spend most of my time guiding tourists to my ancestral places such as Chichen-Itza, Mayapan, Yaxuma, Chakumputun, Tulum and Coba.

I am now approaching my sixth decade on this planet. Most of my adult life has been spent in the United States. In 2007, I was allowed to "voluntarily depart" the U.S., yet I yearn to return. Whenever I leave, my father asks why I go. I tell him "Padre, me tengo que ir," or Father, I must go.

Soy amigo del veinto y el hijo de la Yucatan. I am a friend of the wind and a son of the Yucatan. I love my family, my country, my people, my heritage, my ancestry and all that I am, have been and will be. My father asks me why I would leave all that I have and go to a country that does not want me. This is what I tell him. This is my story.

Jorge Frias

Prologue

One day, as I was sitting on a bench in a park in Seattle, drinking a cup of coffee I had just bought from a Starbucks, overlooking the waters of the Puget Sound and watching people come off ferry boats, I saw a group of over a dozen uniformed law enforcement officers of some kind get off a boat and come walking towards me. Their offices were two floors above the Starbucks and they had to walk right past me to get to the building. Being paranoid about having police officers anywhere near me, I tried to think of a way I could leave without drawing attention to myself. It all happened so fast there was nothing I could do except sit there and act as normally as I could.

I saw from their uniforms that they were all U.S. Customs and Immigration agents. Every one of them walked within a few feet of me. They all said hello to me and I said hello right back to them. I had a tour book of the Seattle area in my hands and I kept my head down, pretending to be reading it. The last two were older than the others. They seemed to be the ones in charge.

One of the two older men stopped and started to talk to me in Spanish. He asked where I was from and I told him Michigan, since that is where I had come from and I was carrying a valid Michigan driver's license. He asked me what I was doing in Seattle. I told him I was just visiting and that I had never been there before. He wanted to know what I did in Michigan, how long I was staying in Seattle, where I was staying, what I was doing while there and all kinds of things, like he knew that I was an illegal Mexican working without proper papers, which I was, of course, and he was just waiting for me to say the wrong thing and give him an excuse to arrest me.

He asked his questions in a nice, friendly way, but every time I answered a question he had another one for me. After answering the tenth question, I looked down at my cup, saw that it was nearly empty and said that I needed to get a re-fill. I stood, excused myself, and walked towards the Starbucks. He followed me into the store, still talking to me all the while.

I asked the woman at the counter for a re-fill and for some other things, like a roll or pastry which needed to be cooked or heated up, anything that would take her a little time to get. I then asked if they had a restroom. She pointed to where it was and I told her I would be right back.

Once I was inside the restroom, I looked for another way to get out and noticed that there was an emergency exit at the back of the room. I didn't know if the alarm would go off if I used it or not, but I was getting out of there one way or another. When I pushed open the door, fortunately, no bells went off, or at least none that I heard. I took off running down an alley and past some railroad tracks, as fast as I could. I went back to the bus station and got on the first bus back out to the Valley and the ranch where I was working. When you are an illegal, you have to be very careful all of the time.

Chapter One

El Norte

I first came to the United States when I was fourteen years old. I was a passenger in a car driven by my uncle, Otto Munoz, who lived in Chicago. We drove from Progreso, Mexico to Chicago, Illinois in six days. At the time, I didn't think much of it. I wasn't old enough to know that there were laws preventing people from traveling from Mexico to the United States without proper papers.

Uncle Otto was employed by Nabisco and he had worked his way up the ranks of the factory to become a supervisor. He had lived in Chicago for 35 years and had become a citizen of the United States after working for many years with a green card. I'm sure my parents obtained a passport and a visa for me, but I don't recall any of that.

We drove in a new Gran Torino. Few people in Progreso had cars as nice. He had paid taxes in the U.S. for years and was vested in the social security system. He owned a house and was legal in every way, as were his wife and children who were born there. I didn't speak much English but after spending several weeks that summer with him and his family, which consisted of his wife and four young children, all younger than me, I learned to speak much better.

Getting into the United States and back was no problem. Uncle Otto took care of everything. When I returned to Progreso with new blue jeans, a Chicago Cubs t-shirt and black Converse basketball shoes I felt very special. I realized at that early age that the U.S. offered many products that weren't available to me in Mexico.

On our way to and from Chicago we stayed with a cousin, Jenny, who lived in Brownsville, Texas. Two summers later, in the summer of my sixteenth year, I went back to stay with her again. Through her, I got a job working in a brick factory doing manual work, carrying bricks and other things. My hours were from 8 to 5, five days per week and I worked for less than two months. They paid me $4.25 per hour and by the time I left Brownsville and returned to Progreso for my last year in high school, I had earned over a thousand dollars, which was an enormous amount of money for me. I don't remember it, but I must have used the passport and visa from two years before. I was still just a kid and my parents made all the arrangements.

That was my first taste of the American Dollar, and I liked it. America was the land of opportunity. I knew that the United States offered an opportunity to earn more money and do more things than anyplace or anything I would find in Progreso, the Yucatan or Mexico. I would be back to America again, it was just a matter of time.

I also met my first American girl then. She was a tall, thin, blonde, green-eyed beauty named Carol and I immediately fell madly in love with her. She and I wrote back and forth to each other for the rest of that year on a near-daily basis. Long distance phone calls were expensive back then, much more than now, but we would talk to each other on Sunday nights, when the rates were the lowest, for fifteen or twenty minutes. The romance died on the vine sometime during the winter, but it left a big impression on me.

My uncle and his wife, Auntie Elba, and their four children, moved to Houston a few years later, when Uncle Otto retired from the factory. He wanted to stay in the United States but be as close to Mexico as possible, and Texas was as close as he could get.

I graduated from high school in 1979 but, although it beckoned, "El Norte" would have to wait. I decided to learn about things like hotel management and tourism services. I figured that would be the best way for me to find a good job in the U.S. and I planned to get into that type of business at some level and work my way up.

My parents supported my decision to go to college. That was expected of me. My father, who is a very smart man, wanted me to follow in his footsteps. He would have preferred that I study journalism or history. I had an interest in journalism and I inherited from him a love of literature in general and poetry in particular. I began writing poems at an early age and I attribute whatever talents I have in that regard to him and to my mother. The bonds between us run deep.

I didn't have the courage, or the money, to set out on my own. I knew that more education would provide me with a better life in the United States. I also knew that I would need money to make my way in the States. A successful life in the United States wasn't just my goal. I considered it to be my destiny.

I have one brother, Romeo, who is five years older than me. I also have an older sister, Juliet, who is two years older than me. During my last year in high school, my parents surprised me, and themselves, with another daughter, Lilly Rose, who is seventeen years younger than me. When I graduated from high school, Juliet was in her third year of college, in Merida, studying to become a teacher. She had no desire to leave the Yucatan then and she has never left the Yucatan. She is happy there. Romeo, however, was a different story.

After he graduated from high school, Romeo went to the United States on a green card and became a helicopter technician. He lived in Detroit. He married an American woman not long after and had two children with her. He became a citizen with no trouble whatsoever in no time at all.

It had been so easy for Romeo, and for Otto before him, and Aunt Jenny as well, that I never thought I would have any problem at all getting into the United States, getting a good job and becoming an American citizen. That was a given. It was just a matter of when that would happen, not if.

So I enrolled in the school of business at the Institute of Technology in Merida. During the summer months and during holidays I took tourists to the various Mayan archeological sites closest to home. My father had friends in the business and one of them gave me a job. Tourism had become a profitable enterprise. With improved technology and aerial photography, more and more Mayan ruins were being discovered and excavated. The Mexican government was spending substantial amounts of money restoring the temples at the time. Being a guide forced me to learn how to speak English better. I also learned to speak some French, Italian and other languages as well. I was taught how to be a photographer. Tourists loved getting photographs of themselves at temples and they paid handsomely for them.

The people I met on those guide trips, especially in the early days, were usually bright, curious, adventurous and full of life. I enjoyed listening to them tell of all the things they had done and all the places they had been. People who traveled from faraway places to see Mayan temples and learn about my Mayan ancestors were of great interest to me. I wanted to be like them some day.

I was a good student, though not particularly motivated to graduate in a hurry. I enjoyed the classes I took and took great care in choosing the classes to take. There were several years when I only took a few courses. Early on I learned that good teachers were more important than a great class. Good teachers made even dull subjects interesting whereas dull teachers could ruin even the most interesting of subjects. My sister helped me in finding out who the best teachers were.

I worked with my father in the newspaper business from a very early age. Many of his printing presses and other machines were in our home and newspapers and articles and books he was working on or reading were always strewn all over the house. Though I balked at taking the bit and joining him and his brother in the business, I was never too far from it or from him. I worshiped my father. I still do.

To encourage me, he would publish many of the articles I wrote. I took an interest in the Progreso political scene and attended meetings of the city council on a regular basis. When I did, I wrote reports of what I saw and heard and what I thought about things. My father gave me wide latitude and allowed me much freedom of expression, even when he disagreed with me, and I appreciated that.

But what dominated my time and my interest during those years was the main passion in my life, and that was soccer. I enjoyed covering and writing about the sporting scene in Progreso, Merida and the Yucatan. In doing so, I gained some recognition for that.

However, ever since I was old enough to walk, as far back as I can remember, I played soccer. I loved playing the game. My best memories from my childhood are of those days of playing soccer. My parents, and especially my father, supported me in that, too. My father understood my passion for the game much more than my mother did. My mother always wanted to see me do well, and she loved seeing me happy, but to her it was just a game that I would eventually outgrow. I don't think my father ever missed a game.

My parents' house, the only home I have ever known, sits across from the plaza in the middle of downtown Progreso. It has a modest, unassuming entrance, with little more than a door and a name-plate on the wall. Once inside, it goes back a hundred feet and has a large courtyard in the middle with a bedroom, my bedroom, in the back. An eight foot high concrete wall separated our house from the building next to us on the west side. My father's brother, Uncle Ramon, lived there. They worked together in the newspaper business for years and were very close.

On the other side was a movie theatre and the wall was over twenty feet high. There was no roof over the top of our courtyard. If I had a peso for every soccer ball I kicked into or over those walls I would be a rich man. I learned early on to kick towards the movie theatre, though my uncle always threw my ball back without protest.

I have a short, sturdy body and I have always been a fast runner. I have very wide feet, as is characteristic of Mayans. In fact, that trait of having big feet is called "piez de Indio," or feet of the Indians. I started playing on teams in organized play at age eight and I was a very good player right from the start.

The elementary schools I attended were less than a hundred yards away from my house and the playgrounds were always open to us after school was over. My friends and I played soccer, or juego del futbol, as we called it, endlessly.

There are many things that are different between the United States and Mexico and recreational programs and facilities are among them. In Mexico, we had a little league baseball league that we all played in but other than that soccer was our only activity. Most of our soccer games were played on the playgrounds at school, not in formal leagues. I participated in every organized soccer activity that was available to me.

On Sundays, the local towns would play each other and people would come to watch. When I was younger, my father and I would go together and watch. When I was old enough, I joined the team.

Jorge as a teenager in Progreso.

Most of the cities had teams and I played for Progreso's men's team when I was in my early teens. I played on that team for many years, even after I had moved away, as long as it didn't conflict with another league I was in. It was the closest thing to professional soccer we had, outside of Mexico City or any of the larger metropolitan areas, like Monterrey, Tampico or Vera Cruz. Everybody knew me, at least in Progreso, and I was known throughout the Yucatan, too, as a good player.

Whenever someone organized a team from the state of the Yucatan to play against either of the other two states in the Yucatan region, Quintana Roo and Campeche, or against any of the other states in the country, I was always chosen to be part of the team. I wanted very badly to be on the team that represented Mexico in the World Cup or the Olympics, and I was good enough to be given an opportunity to try out for those teams.

In 1981, when I was in my early twenties, I went to Mexico City and played with the reserves for the Mexican Olympic team. We practiced with the men on the team that played in the 1982 World Cup. The Olympics were to be played in 1984. I, like all of the other guys on that "reserve" team, hoped that someone would retire or that an opportunity would present itself so that I would be able to get a spot on the big team. I played on the best field in all of Mexico, la Estadio Azteca, Aztec Stadium, many times. I dreamed of being a star. That never happened for me, though a few of the guys I played with on that reserve team made the Olympic team a few years later.

I played on the team at my college, the Technologico de Merida, every year I was allowed to play. It wasn't like the United States though, where you had the National Collegiate Athletic Association sponsoring a major year-end tournament to decide a national champion, with games televised on ESPN. Our team did well and had a winning record every year. During those years, I lived and breathed soccer every day.

In 1987 I was selected to play for Club Aguilas, a third division professional team, and was paid money to play. That was the highest level of soccer I ever played. I stayed in the Yucatan for almost ten years after high school just so that I could play soccer. My position was forward and my job was to score goals, and I did.

Since I wasn't as tall as many of the defenders, I had to beat them with my speed to the ball. My name was in the paper often, and not just in the papers published by my father, but that was what my friends would tell me, especially when I got my picture in the paper.

Injuries are part of the game and I had my share of them. I sprained ankles and twisted knees many times. I was carried off the field several times but I was fortunate in that regard. I was never so seriously injured that I was unable to get back to the game without missing too many days. I did whatever I had to do so that I could play. I loved it. But because of various nicks and bruises, I spent a lot of time in whirlpools and with trainers and massage therapists, as most of the other guys did as well.

In 1988, after almost eight years in college, I was ready to graduate. I had every intention of continuing to play soccer until they tore my uniform off of me, but unless I decided to go to graduate school, my college days were near the end. However, my life changed quite unexpectedly one spring day during my last year of college.

I was walking on the beach in Progreso at sunset. I was looking down, deep in thought, not paying attention to where I was going. I saw something out of the corner of my eye, looked up, and came to an abrupt stop. I had almost run right into a tall, thin, green-eyed woman with long, blonde hair.

She hadn't been paying attention to where she was going either and she was as startled to see me as I her. We exchanged apologies and laughed at what had almost happened. We introduced ourselves. Her name was Mary. She was by herself and had a cigarette in her hand. I asked if I could have one and she obliged. She told me that she and some friends were vacationing from Canada and that they were looking forward to seeing Mayan temples. I told her that I was a guide and could take them. Our conversation continued and became more animated.

We walked back along the beach towards the Pelicano's Hotel, where she and her friends were staying. For part of the way, we walked on the mile long boardwalk which ran alongside the beach, called the Malecon. Though my English was not very good, her Spanish was no better. We struggled through, communicating as best we could, anxiously trying to learn more about the other.

The Malecon, Progreso

We talked for the next two hours until the sky was completely dark, long after the sun had gone down. It was a clear night and a full moon came up which provided a romantic backdrop to what had become a magical evening for both of us. Neither of us gave a thought to having dinner, or even anything to drink. She seemed to be enjoying my company as much as I was enjoying hers. We found a spot on the beach across from her hotel and talked more. After four or five hours, I kissed her good night and went home.

Early the next morning, I was up and on the beach, right outside her hotel, hoping to see her again. After a couple of hours, she and her friends came down to the beach near where I was sitting. She was with an older woman and two young children. They were looking for a house to rent for a month. Mary was the baby-sitter.

She introduced me to Judy and her two children. I offered to help them find a house to rent, guide them to and through the Mayan temples and do whatever I could to make their stay more enjoyable. I would have done anything they asked to keep me close to Mary. I found a house for them a few blocks away, right across the street from the Gulf and from the Malecon. I helped them move from their hotel into the house and spent the entire day with them.

Later that afternoon, Mary and I went for another long walk, once she was able to leave the children and get some time to herself. Our mutual attraction grew stronger that day and every day after that. After they had been there for a week, Judy asked me to take them to some Mayan temples and teach them about the Mayan civilization.

Over the next several weeks, I took them to Chichen-Itza, Uxmal, Kabah, Dzibilichalton, Izamal and Labna, among others. Each one was a separate trip. All were within a two hour drive of Progreso. Each was different from the others in some significant way.

Mary was nineteen and I was twenty six. She had graduated from high school and was trying to decide what she wanted to do with her life. At first, I think she was more excited about the fact that she had met a real Mexican and was learning to speak Spanish. I'm sure she was also happy to have a native teach her all about the Mayans and Mexican culture, too, but there was more to it than that. There was romance between us.

For me, it was all about Mary. Nothing was more important than being with her. Not school, not my job, not soccer, nothing. She was my first real love. I had romantic interests over the years, but nothing like her before. I knew that I was in love and I told her so. We made love to each other for the first time on a blanket on the beach a few days before she left.

When it came time for her to go, I was distraught. I didn't want her to leave and she didn't want to go. We both cried as she boarded the Ado bus in Merida to head back to Silver City, New Mexico, where her family lived.

We swore to stay in touch and that we'd get together as soon as we could. Not long after she was back in the States Mary moved to Denver to work in a restaurant. She started saving money to come back to Mexico and I turned my attention back to completing my last year of college.

By the time I graduated, which was in June of 1988, I had decided that if we were going to stay in Mexico that Cancun was where we should live. It had grown dramatically in the ten plus years since it had come into existence and there were plenty of opportunities for me to make money, much more so than in Progreso or Merida, and there was no doubt whatsoever about that. There were more tourists and more businesses in Cancun than Progreso had ever seen, many more.

Cancun and Playa del Carmen had become like the Disneyland I had heard of but never seen. Every day was a carnival. Each day tourists arrived, replacing the ones who left. It was a revolving door of tourists, all with money to spend and little reluctance to spend it.

After Cancun first opened, which was in the mid to late '70s, as the tourists began to discover it, fewer tourists came to Progreso. Some still came, but not nearly as many as before Cancun was created. Every year fewer and fewer people came to Progreso. By 1988, tourists rarely came to Progreso at all. It didn't have a single hotel to match the splendor of any of the many magnificent and enormous resorts being created by Hilton, Ritz-Carlton and all the rest. The rise of Cancun had been the death knell for Progreso.

Mary wanted to be in Mexico with me. When I suggested that we should live in Cancun instead of Progreso she readily agreed. I wanted to have enough money saved up so that when Mary came down we could get a nice place to live and have enough money for us to have a good time, too. We were both working with a purpose and a plan.

We wrote to each other on a near daily basis. I called as often as money would permit. I wrote poems to her and about her. Our love for each other was strong and growing stronger.

I rented an apartment in Cancun, not far from the water but far enough so that the rent wasn't more than we could afford. I bought a 22 foot boat with a 25 horsepower Evinrude motor on the back that could carry up to six tourists on snorkeling and fishing trips. I was still working as a guide taking people to the temples whenever I was asked to do so.

One of my friends was a tour operator who called me whenever he had more people signed up than he could handle by himself. He had two vans and I would drive one and he would drive the other. Usually we took people to either Tulum or Coba, and most of the time we went to the same place, but sometimes he'd go to one temple and I'd go to the other.

At night, I worked at a hamburger stand which I had constructed, selling Mexican hamburgers with guacamole and salsa to the gringos as they left the discos. I told them it was a Mexican cure to prevent a hangover. I was working seven days a week. I was making more money than ever. Mary was planning to join me once the summer season ended in Denver, which was only weeks away, and I was ready for her.

On September 14, 1988, just before Mary was to arrive, Hurricane

Gilbert put an end to all of our plans. What was supposed to be a mild storm, with little to fear, turned out to be a killer storm. It claimed the lives of 341 people and caused an estimated $5.5 billion U.S. dollars of damage. It was reportedly the largest storm in history up to that time. The storm measured 500 nautical miles in diameter. Its highest winds, measured over a full minute of sustained gusts, were calculated to be 185 miles per hour.

35,000 people were reportedly left homeless in the Yucatan before Gilbert finally turned north and went up into Texas, Oklahoma and Kansas days later. I was one of them. 60,000 homes were destroyed. 83 ships were sunk.

My boat was destroyed, my hamburger stand went with the wind, and my apartment was uninhabitable. It would take months, if not years, to rebuild Cancun. When I called Mary to tell her what had happened and that I had lost everything, her immediate response was that I should come to Colorado. I agreed.

I got a passport from Mexican authorities without any problem whatsoever. To obtain a visa I had to go to the U.S. Consulate in Merida. Getting the visa was not as easy as I had hoped, however. Not that I posed a problem for American security, it was the administrative web of paperwork that baffled and bothered me. I wasn't able to adequately answer all of the questions asked of me, such as how long I would be there, what I would do while there, where I would stay and all those things. It was time-consuming and I had no time to wait. I was in a hurry.

Finally, out of sheer frustration after days of failure and ineptitude, I sought the assistance of one of my professors at the Technological College in Merida who knew the American Consul. He made a phone call to her on my behalf and, though she was leaving that very day to return to the States for some reason, she personally saw to it that my application was processed. In fact, she waited for me as I literally ran several miles through the streets of Merida to get to her office before it closed. She gave me a visa that was good for ten years. Little did I know at the time how valuable that would be for me in the years ahead. I had no idea that most visas were usually issued for six months at a time, a year at most. She had done me a great favor.

A few days after that I was aboard an Aero Mexico plane on my way from Merida to Houston and then on to Denver, where I went through Customs. The Immigration officer wanted to know what I planned to do in the United States since I had no green card allowing me to work while there. I told him I was on vacation and that Mary was there to meet me. He called her into the office and required her to confirm for him that I would be staying with her before allowing me through customs. He even asked her, because she looked so young and innocent, if her mother knew what she was doing. He thought about calling her mother but, after over an hour, he reluctantly let me in.

Once I exited the airport to the sight of the Rocky Mountains filling the skies to the west, in a car Mary borrowed from her mother, the carnage of Hurricane Gilbert quickly became a distant memory. Mary and I were together and, in what seemed like an instant, I was in America, fulfilling my dreams of many years before. The business of a green card or a work permit were of no consequence to me. I hadn't thought that far ahead. I hadn't planned any of this.

Mary lived in an apartment in Denver which her mother had rented where Mary, her older sister and a brother lived. Her mother had a house in Silver City and spent most of her time in New Mexico, but when I arrived her mother was there at the apartment in Denver. There was a small room in the front where I was supposed to sleep. I always found a way into Mary's bedroom during the night but I'd be back in my room by morning.

Within a few days of my arrival, I had offers to work at my choice of three different restaurants, thanks to Mary's recommendations. The restaurants all served Mexican food and catered to what was a large Hispanic population. When asked for a social security number, I gave them nine numbers. That satisfied them. I began as a dish washer at a restaurant called La Cantina, not far from downtown Denver.

Mary was a waitress at a fancy restaurant not far from where I worked. We went to work together in her car and drove home together, though she often had to wait for me to get off, since I had to do clean up and close the restaurant, which she didn't have to do. She didn't mind. Sometimes I'd meet her at one of the bars nearby where we'd have a beer or two and listen to music before heading home.

On our off-days we hiked in the Rocky Mountains as often as we could, camped in tents in the national parks, and canoed and kayaked the rivers in Southern Colorado and northern New Mexico. We worked hard and played hard, saving what money we could along the way.

For eight months, our love for each other blossomed. We spoke of getting married. Those were the best days of my life. I loved her very much but, as things turned out, apparently she didn't love me quite as much as I loved her.

It all started to unravel when Mary's wanderlust and my lack of proper papers separated us. She loved the outdoors and wild places as much I did, and maybe even more. The next summer, that being the summer of 1989, we talked of leaving Colorado and going to Alaska to see the northern lights and explore the Arctic wilderness. Mary would have no problem at all getting a job there. I was concerned that I wouldn't be able to get in, let alone find a job, because I didn't have a green card.

My Visa allowed me to travel and I could come and go as I pleased for ten years if I wanted to. It was just that I wasn't allowed to work on that visa, so I couldn't get a job without getting a green card or a work permit. In Denver, where there were so many Mexicans, most of whom were probably illegal, like me, I had no trouble at all, but in Alaska, where there were probably very few Hispanics, I was sure that no one would hire me.

Also, going from Colorado to Alaska meant getting on an airplane, since we didn't want to drive all that way. Besides, even if we drove, I'd have to clear customs in Canada and then do it again when re-entering the United States in Alaska. I wanted to avoid any law enforcement officials altogether. I was sure that someone would ask what I had been doing in Colorado for the last eight months and what I would be doing in Alaska. No one would believe that I was a rich man with an unlimited budget who had been on vacation all that time. I was afraid to take a chance that I would be sent back to Mexico.

I thought about applying for a green card then but the problem was that if I did that and told the U.S. government where I'd been and what I'd been doing, I was sure that I would be deported. I had been working illegally for over eight months. I wasn't the only one in that situation. I'd met hundreds and hundreds of people in that exact same situation.

Nobody knew what the U.S. government would do with illegals and nobody wanted to find out. Everybody knew people who had been caught and sent back. Everyone knew to stay under the radar and not attract any attention. I decided it was best for me to stay in Denver and wait for her to get back. I moved in with one of the other guys I worked with who had an apartment close to where we worked. Mary said I could have stayed at her mother's house but I wasn't comfortable with that.

So Mary left for Alaska without me at the beginning of Alaska's summer season in early June of 1989. We thought it was only going to be a temporary thing and that she'd be home by August, when the summer season ended, since it only lasts a few months in Alaska. During those months, things changed.

We wrote to each other regularly and spoke to each other daily. Our plan was to meet in Vermont, where her brother was in medical school. He was graduating and it was a big family affair. I was invited and I would be welcome. Her family loved me, too.

I knew something was wrong when she suggested during a telephone conversation that it might be better if I didn't go. She said things like she didn't want me to spoil the occasion if I got caught, because I was an illegal alien. I went anyway. I was in love with her and hadn't seen her in almost three months. I hungered to see her again, and as soon as possible. I couldn't wait until she got back to Colorado.

Things went badly in Vermont. As soon as I saw her face I could tell that things were different. When we embraced, it wasn't the same. When we had a chance to talk privately, she said that we should stop seeing each other for a while. The next few days were awkward. When it was time to go she made it official. Our relationship was over, according to her. It ended as it began, quite suddenly. For me, it ended badly as that was not my decision and that was not what I wanted.

I went straight from Vermont to be with my brother in Michigan. I was distraught, damaged goods. With Romeo and his family, I was protected by a family umbilical cord and I planned to stay inside that womb for a while. I swore that I would never return to Denver, not even to get my clothes and other belongings, though while I was in Michigan, I called her a few times. She told me not to call her again. In a quiet moment, I wrote a poem which conveyed my feelings.

Sadness

What is life without sadness?
It always arrives without a greeting;
It goes without saying good bye;
It causes us to stumble in the night;
It makes us pray to our God;
Though happiness and joy are just a step away,
Sadness doesn't allow you to see them;
It makes you cry and it cries with you;
It allows you to find loves that have been hidden,
And, over time, it gives hope that you will find love and be loved.

Chapter Two

On the Radar Screen

My brother found me a job working for a friend of his laying sod and doing landscape work at a new housing complex in a small town called Oxford, not far from the Canadian border, an hour from Detroit. I was not doing well emotionally and my brother and his wife helped me get through. It was the worst time of my life up to that point.

All of the other men I worked with were from Mexico, too, and I thought that they were all probably illegals, just like me, though I never talked about it with any of them. I felt that the less people knew about me the better, even those who I befriended and thought I could trust. In fact, I figured it would be better for them if they didn't know I was an illegal. If they knew, and they helped me, they could get in trouble themselves.

When I wasn't working, I liked to go fishing in Lake Michigan or in any of the many lakes within an hour drive of Lake Orion, where my brother lived. When the cold weather came and the landscaping business ended, I found a job washing dishes at the Sagebrush Cantina, which served Mexican food. Most of the patrons were Hispanics. While there, they let me wait tables and I made more money than I would have as a dishwasher or busboy. Most of the patrons spoke Spanish, but my English was improving and I was able to communicate with everyone with little difficulty.

I stayed with my brother and his family through that winter. I had nowhere else to go, other than going back to Progreso, but I wasn't ready to return home, defeated. I felt safe with Romeo and his family. Inside, I was still hurting.

I saved enough money that winter to buy a used Chevrolet Chevette from one of my fellow employees. When spring came, I told my brother I was going to travel and see America. He didn't want to let me leave because he knew I was still not thinking clearly. He also knew that, although my visa and passport were good, I was an illegal and if I was caught working anywhere I could be put in jail and deported, which was true. I went anyway.

Before I left, with my brother's help, I obtained a Michigan driver's license, giving them my brother's address, copies of pay stubs and a library card or something. I don't remember. I had no trouble getting it. I had no trouble buying the car or insurance, either. Romeo helped me with that, too. Everything was legal, but I think I had to list my brother as a co-owner on some things and that may have been why it went so smoothly.

In April of 1990, once the snow had melted, though I had no green card and no work permit, I headed out to see America. I went toward Maryland first because my cousin, Gabriel, Uncle Otto and Aunt Elba's oldest child, was working as a landscaper in a small town about 40 miles outside of Baltimore. He was an American citizen, having been born in Chicago. He was all grown up at twenty three years old, on his own, with a job, making money and supporting himself.

Gabriel was, like me, planning to travel around and see America. Ironically, he was planning on going to Alaska when it was warm enough, which he could do, since he was a citizen and had the papers, with no problem at all. I stayed with him through the early summer until he left for Alaska. When he left, I shared a house with some of my fellow laborers.

On my days off I went into Washington, D.C. and saw the museums and monuments. I also went to Annapolis to see the Naval Academy. While there, I bought a windsurfing board and surfed on Chesapeake Bay. I canoed the Potomac River and hiked the surrounding Blue Ridge Mountains out near Luray, Virginia, by myself.

My heart was still mending from the loss of Mary. I learned to accept the solitude of being alone as a part of life. I wrote poems about what it felt like. It was a new experience for me, being alone that is. I would have rather been with Mary. I would have taken her back in a heart-beat, but that wasn't something that was within my control. Once Gabriel left for Alaska, I had no family with me in Maryland after he left and a few acquaintances, no friends. I was alone in America, except when I was with my family. I wrote a poem about how I felt.

Loneliness

I walk with sonnets in my brain on foggy nights;
I walk without purpose, but without getting lost;
Loneliness is with me
We walk like companions;
It protects me from the cold wind;
And it prevents me from feeling alone

I liked the D.C. area and decided to stay there for a while. After Gabriel left for Alaska, I quit the landscaping job and went to work for a road building company doing mostly manual labor, like digging up asphalt and re-surfacing parking lots. I was paid much more money than I ever made in restaurants, the factory or doing landscaping, but the work was much harder. I had to be up at 5:30 and I worked long hours, usually getting home after dark.

One day we were working at the General Hospital in Washington, D.C., re-doing a parking lot. I was working with a jack-hammer which was as big as I was. I was digging up the old lot that was being replaced. I was wearing a helmet, heavy gloves and protection for my eyes, like I was supposed to, but none of that was of any help when a large piece of rebar or wire mesh came flying out of the ground and hit me just above my right lip.

The metal went through my lip, through the gums of my teeth, and into the bone. I was knocked to the ground and was barely conscious. When I got to my feet, I saw my reflection in the window of a nearby car and there was blood everywhere. My fellow workers took me to our supervisor who immediately took me to the emergency room of the hospital.

I had never been in an American hospital before and I was more worried about being caught and put out of the country than I was about how badly I'd been injured. My supervisor waited with me and did most of the talking for me. I was still bleeding profusely. I was holding a bloody towel to my lip to slow the loss of blood and couldn't talk too well. The woman at the counter put my name in the computer, using my name and the social security number I'd given the construction company. She soon determined that the information didn't match. She told my supervisor that the hospital wasn't going to be able to take care of me until the problem was straightened out.

I knew the social security number was wrong but there was nothing I could do about it, since I also knew I didn't have a valid number to give them. I didn't know what else they had in the computer on me so I just played the part of an ignorant construction worker. I told them that the mistake must have been on their end and insisted that she had the correct number.

I sat there, in pain, continuing to lose blood, as she took care of other people and waited for updated information from the Social Security Administration, which wasn't going to happen. My supervisor became impatient and kept asking when I would receive some medical attention, saying that the company would pay the bill if the insurance company wouldn't.

I watched as doctors and nurses passed by, knowing that any of them could help me by at least cleaning the wound and giving me some pain medication. I would have been happy with that. I wanted out of there.

I sat there for hours. My supervisor stayed with me most of the time but every now and then he had to leave to attend to another emergency. I began to recognize several of the doctors as they passed by me time and time again. Most didn't even look over at me or make eye contact. This one doctor who passed by many times over the span of those several hours was friendly to me and some of the other patients who were waiting to get in to see a doctor. He offered some words of greeting, or consolation, saying that it shouldn't be too much longer, things like that.

Finally, after he passed by me for the twentieth time over a three hour span he asked me what the problem was and I told him. He made an inquiry at the front desk about my situation. When he found out that the reason I wasn't being seen was that the insurance company hadn't approved treatment, he must have figured out, or at least suspected, that

I was an illegal and that was why my information wasn't coming up in the system. He said, "Come with me," and he took me back into one of the triage rooms, where doctors and nurses do an initial examination of the problem.

As he was examining me, with my supervisor standing right next to him, he asked me where I was from and I told him the Yucatan. He brightened at that and told me how he had just returned from a trip to Cancun. It might have been his honeymoon. I can't remember.

We talked about Cozumel, Tulum and other places he had been and things he had seen and done while in the Yucatan, though he did most of the talking, and then he walked me over to another department. He told me that he was taking me to see the best oral surgeon in the hospital. He also said that the man was one of the best doctors in the entire metropolitan area, if not the country, as well.

I was given some antibiotics and a shot of morphine before even seeing the doctor. In fact, by the time I was taken to see the oral surgeon I was sedated to the point where I now have a vague recollection of seeing a man with a surgical mask over his face and a white bandana of some kind on his head, with huge white gloves on, putting stitches in my lip. Seven hours after being injured, I was released from the hospital. I was given a prescription for more antibiotics and pain medications and told to return in ten days to have the stitches removed, unless a problem developed before then.

It was late summer and I wasn't going to be able to work for a few weeks. I knew that the problem with the social security number wasn't going to go away and I figured that the problem could only get worse for me, the legal problem that is, not the medical problem. I decided to go to Miami to visit my Auntie Elba. We could take the stitches out ourselves if we had to.

By that time, which was the summer of 1990, Uncle Otto had died and Aunt Elba had moved to Miami. She chose Miami because she liked being close to the water and she wasn't that fond of Texas. She said she never cared too much for Houston and she was never going back to those cold Chicago winters. A week or so later, after getting all of the money owed me from the construction company, I put everything I owned in the Chevette and headed south, without going back to the hospital or seeing another doctor.

My Auntie Elba lived in the northwestern part of Miami, out in the Miami Gardens area. Her son Manny, who was in his early twenties, was living with her. He was working at a restaurant on South Beach and told me he could get me a job with no problem at all.

I didn't want to be in public when I first arrived because I was very self-conscious about the scar on my face. It was going to take a long time for that to heal. After a few weeks of hiding inside their apartment, I went to work at the restaurant where he was working, washing dishes, cleaning tables, vacuuming the restaurant, doing whatever they wanted me to do, and avoiding people as much as I could.

Just getting into and out of the restaurant exposed me to the night life of South Beach, which was not like anyplace I'd ever been. There were so many beautiful young people, all of whom were looking to have a good time. They all seemed to have lots of money to spend. It was like a permanent spring-break. Cancun had become a place for thousands and thousands of college kids to come during their week off in the spring, so I was no stranger to a party atmosphere, but South Beach was like that every day and every night, non-stop, and more of it. Miami Beach was a much bigger city than Cancun.

When I wasn't working, I found places where people played soccer and there were many such places in the area. There were many people from Honduras, Guatemala, El Salvador, Columbia, Costa Rica, Nicaragua and Mexico…from all over, who loved to play soccer as I did. There were organized leagues with paid referees. The teams wore uniforms and everything, but it wasn't well-publicized and nobody came to watch except for family and friends. There was a good field at Flamingo Park on Alton Road and 12th Street where I liked to play when kids weren't playing American football on it.

I didn't mind playing soccer with guys with my mouth looking like it did and, after a while, I became less self conscious and started feeling as if I could mingle with women again. I started by having a few beers with Manny and his friends after work. Of course, that could be five o'clock in the morning sometimes. Music didn't start until midnight on some nights and it wasn't unusual for me to be closing the restaurant at two or three o'clock and then going out to have beers. It was nothing like Colorado, Michigan or Maryland or anyplace else I'd been to in the U.S. There were hundreds of beautiful women parading up and down the boulevard and in the bars, but I was still hurting from Mary and I was sure that they weren't looking for me.

South Beach was the home to many movie stars at the time, like Madonna and Sylvester Stallone, and many more stars came to visit. Whenever a professional sporting team came to Miami to play the Heat, the Dolphins, the Panthers or the Marlins, some of the athletes would always show up in South Beach after the game was over. I recognized some of the stars but there were so many it seemed as if everybody was a star, or they thought they were. Everybody was out strutting their stuff for all the world to see. I was a nobody, but I was there with them.

I'd heard of Mickey Rourke and I'd seen one or two of his movies. He owned a bar there and we went to it every now and then. He was one of the big stars on the strip. I would've recognized him if I saw him, but I never saw him.

One night, I was having a beer after work with Manny and his friends at a little place called the News Café where some guys were playing jazz. I was standing there, minding my own business, and all of a sudden there was a guy standing a few feet away from me who was ready to beat up the bartender for some reason.

The bartender, whose name was Nelson, was a friend of Manny's and Manny was standing between me and this other guy. Manny and a bunch of his friends told this other guy to leave the bar and the guy got real belligerent. I thought a fight was going to take place. I was in no condition to fight anybody and wanted no trouble with the law, so I moved out of the way as fast as I could. The guy left a few minutes later. Afterwards I found out that the guy was one of Mickey Rourke's body guards.

One of the guys who was there, ready to fight for Manny and his friend, was a guy named Matthew Sky. We met that night for the first time. He was an outdoorsman, too, and we talked about places we'd been and things we'd done. He was an athlete, too, and we had things in common. The next day, we went running on the beach together and before long we had become friends. He was a big fisherman and we went fishing together a few times after that.

After I was there in South Beach for several months, Manny told me that he wanted to start a business of buying cars in Miami, driving them back to Mexico and selling them for a profit. He had purchased a Thunderbird and wanted me to go with him to Mexico to sell it. He promised to share some of the profits with me.

I wasn't ready to leave Miami but Manny was my cousin and he was insistent that I go with him. He and his mother had been so nice to me it was hard for me to refuse and, besides, I hadn't been home in almost two years. I wasn't worried about getting back into Mexico. My problem was going to be getting back into the United States if I left.

My passport was still valid and my visa was good for another eight years. I thought it might be a good thing to start over with a new visa entry. Things had gone so easily for me, except for that incident at the hospital, and I had met so many people who were illegal aliens, I was thinking that maybe I wouldn't have a problem at all. I had entered the country legally. I was allowed to be in the country for ten years. Where I would have a problem was if they discovered that I had been working illegally. What would I say if asked what I had done for the last two years? The more I thought about it, the more I didn't want to go, but I was committed and I went.

We crossed the border at Brownsville, Texas, and drove into Mexico with no problem. I thought I was home free, literally, but once inside Mexico we were stopped by the Federales. It was in Mariposa, which is across the border from Brownsville. It had nothing to do with me, but the Federales told us that we had to go back to the United States and get a letter from law enforcement in the U.S. saying that the Thunderbird wasn't a stolen car. I told Manny to go by himself and that I would wait for him to return. He didn't want me to do that and kept telling me not to worry, that I wouldn't have any problem since I had a valid Mexican passport. I didn't want to go, but he insisted.

When we got to the border, the United States Immigration officials wouldn't let me in the country. They saw where I had entered the country in Denver in September of 1988 and now it was 1990. They wanted to know what I had been doing all that time. They didn't believe me when I told them that I had been visiting relatives.

They took all of my information and made me sign a letter saying that I wouldn't return to the U.S. for five years. I did what they told me and signed whatever they put in front of me, but I was pissed at Manny for making me go through that. Now I had been discovered and wouldn't be able to return to the U.S. for five years.

I waited in Mariposa until Manny came back. It took him a while to do the things he had to do and he got there just in time to save me from being robbed and beaten. People at the border towns are different from those anywhere else in Mexico, except maybe some parts of Mexico City. There are many illegal activities going on, such as drug dealing, prostitution, robberies and other street crimes, and there are gangs which prey on tourists, visitors, or even fellow Mexicanos like me, who were out of place. He pulled up just as I was about to get jumped.

We drove the rest of the way back to Progreso with no problem. He sold the Thunderbird for a profit, like he said, but he didn't make as much as he expected so he didn't give me as much as I thought I was going to get. I wished I'd stayed in Miami.

Not long after I was back home, I received a call from someone at the U.S. Consulate in Merida asking me to come see him. He was a big African-American man who had been a player in the National Football League. He asked me many questions about what I had done and where I had gone while in the U.S. and why I hadn't returned for so long. He didn't think any more of my explanation that I was visiting family and friends all that time than the border guards did.

Even though the visa that had been issued to me was still good for several more years, he asked me to surrender it to him. I told him that I had given it to the border guards. He told me that I couldn't return to the U.S. for five years because he wouldn't issue me a visa for five years because of what I'd done.

That was another low point for me because now I was back in Mexico and couldn't go back to the U.S. for five years. After visiting with my family in Progreso for several weeks I decided to go back to Cancun and see if I could start my business again. I could always be a guide and my friend told me that a job was waiting for me whenever I arrived.

Early in the spring of 1991 I returned to Cancun. The tourist season was in full bloom. Being back in Cancun made me think of Mary. I wrote a poem to her, but I never sent it.

Memories

How I miss the love we had for each other;
When that feeling comes, it touches my heart, my

mind, my soul and fills me with gladness;
I miss those times and I don't want to lose them;
I don't want my soul to stay separate from yours,
Our days as companions and lovers are gone, for now;
I still love you deep inside and I don't want those days to be gone forever;
For now, I must let you go, free to travel the road you have chosen to take; as you wish;
Beautiful things await you, I'm sure, and I can only hope that being with me again is one of them.

Jorge back in Cancun

Jorge the photographer

Chapter Three

Boca de Cherna

When I got back to Cancun, things were better than they were when I left but not anywhere near as good as what it had been before Gilbert hit. I started doing guided tours to the temples again and I'd get a snorkeling and dive trip every week or so. I was making enough money to pay for my food, an apartment, a car and still have a little left over at the end of the month. It had been over a year since Mary had broken it off with me and I hadn't fully recovered. The scar on my upper lip was improving, though not yet completely healed. I was feeling better about myself as far as getting out and interacting with people was concerned, but there had been no other women in my life since her.

Of course, my friends took no pity on me and my condition. They called "Boca de Cherrna," which means "mouth of the jewfish." The ironic part of them calling me that name was that I had been called that by some of my classmates when I was a kid, since I have big lips. Whenever they did, I would always fight them. I never liked that name. I still don't, but once my friends found out that I didn't like the name they started calling me that all the more, that or just "Boca D" for short.

It was now the fall of 1991, three years since Gilbert destroyed Cancun. My life was moving along but with no real direction and no passion in it. One day, over some beers after work, one of my friends, Francisco, asked me about sailing a boat with him to Miami. I had been on many sailboats before, but never for more than for an afternoon ride, and the idea of doing that appealed to me. The idea of going to Miami again appealed to me too, even though I knew I would be doing so illegally. It offered me an adventure and I accepted.

I thought that if I could just get into the country I would be okay. My Passport hadn't been revoked and my Michigan driver's license was still valid. I could use my brother's Michigan address, or Aunt Elba's address in Miami, and I had a place to stay in either place if I could only get in. I still had my old visa. I hadn't surrendered it. I knew it was a risk but it was a risk worth taking.

I wanted to be in the United States. I liked living in the United States. It was more exciting to me, much more exciting, than anything I had ever experienced in Progreso, Cancun, Mexico City or anywhere else in Mexico. It wasn't that I didn't love my home or my family, and not that I couldn't make money in Mexico. I could. I knew that. It was because being in America was an adventure. I had been all over the Yucatan and done all the things I wanted to do, like the dive trips, fishing, studying the Mayan civilization and seeing all the temples, but I wanted more adventure in my life. My father said I was too restless, that I was like the wind. He called me el amigo del viento, which means friend of the wind. Some of my friends called me el nino eterna, or the eternal child.

I'm not a stupid person. I have a college degree and I have had more opportunities than most of the people who illegally enter the United States. I knew better than to sneak into the country with a "coyote" across the borders in Texas, New Mexico, Arizona or California, like most of the illegals do, but the process of getting a green card, or trying to become a citizen through the immigration channels, is an extremely lengthy process, usually involving several years of time and effort, and there is never a guarantee that it will be successful. I am impatient and impetuous. I know that about myself. It is not an excuse for my behavior, but it is an explanation. I realize that many people will not accept that from me and I must accept that from them. I am not proud of some of the things I have done in my life, but I never hurt anyone or committed any crimes. I decided to go and take my chances.

I thought to myself, what would they do to me if they caught me? Put me in jail? I didn't think so. They'd send me home. The risk was that I couldn't get another visa for more than five years.

After the decision to sail for Miami with Francisco was made, we started getting the boat ready to make the trip, getting provisions and all the rest. It was a 1981, 35 foot Erwin. Only one person had owned it through all those years and it had been taken good care of. It had a five foot keel and was seaworthy. It had all the newer electronics and a cabin which was high enough I could stand up without hitting my head. There would be three of us on the voyage, Francisco, me and Alex Bravo, another friend of mine.

While getting the boat ready and making preparations for the trip, I enrolled in a course to learn how to sail. If I successfully completed it, I would get a certificate saying that I was a seaman. Though I wouldn't need it with Francisco, it would allow me to get a job down the road if I ever wanted to do that. It seemed like a good idea at the time. The classes were at night, two nights per week for three hours. In six weeks time I learned a lot of useful things about sailing and had a certificate to show for it.

An Italian guy named Marcello and two other men were going to sail a trimaran with us. Once the preparations were made and everything was ready, Francisco made the decision to leave at the beginning of December. A week before we were to leave, the six of us went to a disco place called Cats in Cancun to have a few beers.

We were sitting at a table drinking our beers, listening to a reggae band play Bob Marley music, and watching people dance. Most of the people were tourists. In the middle of the dance floor I saw a tall, thin woman with long red hair.

All of the other men in the bar saw her too. She was a beauty. She stayed on the dance floor most of the night, dancing with one guy after the next. I'm not much of a dancer, and I didn't ask her to dance but I kept an eye on her and every now and then it seemed as if she was looking back at me.

When the band stopped playing for the night, I said my good-byes to my mates and headed out the door. I didn't do anything to cause it to happen, but it just so happened that the red-headed woman and I walked out of the bar, down the steps and onto the street at the same time. I didn't say anything to her and she didn't say anything to me for quite a while, but we walked in the same direction down the street, side-by-side.

After two blocks, as we were still walking together, I said something to her, and I can't remember what it was that I said, but she responded and we started to talk. Her name was Rayna and she was from Canada. She was down for a week on vacation. We talked and talked for the next few blocks until we arrived at the hotel where she was staying. She invited me in and I accepted her invitation. Her mother and the rest of her family were there and it wasn't a romantic kind of thing. We were enjoying each other's company and the conversation and we didn't want it to end. We talked and talked until I fell asleep on her couch.

In the morning, I got up before anyone else was awake. Rayna was asleep somewhere in the apartment, but I never saw her before I left. After writing down the telephone number to her room, I crept out of the apartment as quietly as possible and went to work.

That night, after work, I called her. It was her mother's birthday and she asked me to join them for the celebration. I readily agreed. I saw her that night and for every other day and night until she and her family returned to Canada. We were only together for a week, and we never made love to each other, though there were hugs, kisses and embraces. We created a special bond in that short time. She filled a void in my life. Since Mary and I had separated, no women of interest had entered my life before her. After meeting her I began thinking more and more about her and less and less about Mary as the days went by.

Chapter Four

Oh Beautiful For Spacious Skies

A few days after Rayna had returned to Canada, early one morning, just as the sun was rising, Francisco, Alex and I sailed out of the harbor in Isla de Mujeres headed for Miami. Marcello and his two friends were alongside us. We had a strong wind out of the Northeast in our face so we took a tack that had us headed in the direction of Cuba, at an angle to the wind which allowed us to fill the sails and travel at a good speed.

The trip from Isla de Mujeres to Cabo San Antonio, which is the closest point on the island of Cuba to Mexico, is ninety miles. With that wind filling our sails, we were able to make that leg of the trip in less than two days, which was good time. The whole trip was another three hundred miles, more or less. Key West was a little over eighty miles due north of Cuba, but we would have to sail another two hundred miles or so, or more, after that to get to Miami. Although it was about a hundred miles by car from Key West to Miami we had to sail far out into the Atlantic, almost to Nassau, in order to avoid the reefs, before tacking back into Miami.

Just as the coast of Cuba came into view, we made our tack, the only tack we took on that leg of the trip, for Key West. We had a Loran compass to direct us. The stars were magnificent. It was the first time I had been on the water at night and the view of the night sky, with stars filling the sky from horizon to horizon in all directions, made the trip worthwhile, no matter how it would end.

Yet even in what was as peaceful, beautiful and tranquil a place as any I had ever been in, I felt an emptiness inside me. It was hard for me to understand what it was I was feeling. I should have been ecstatic with joy, but I wasn't. I wrote a poem to express the way I felt that night.

Though filled with the beauty of the waves;
on an endless sea and a clear night sky,
a strange sadness makes me feel lost and out of place;
I look to the sea to find peace;
I look to the skies to find comfort;
I think to myself that the rising sun will be the
beginning of something new and different,
that every day is a journey unto itself;
I think of how many of my days have been filled
with the many wonders of nature;
And how the setting suns brought them to a peaceful and glorious end;
And after the sun had set, while I waited for the sun to
rise again, darkness, much like winter, made me forget
what had been and fear what was to come.

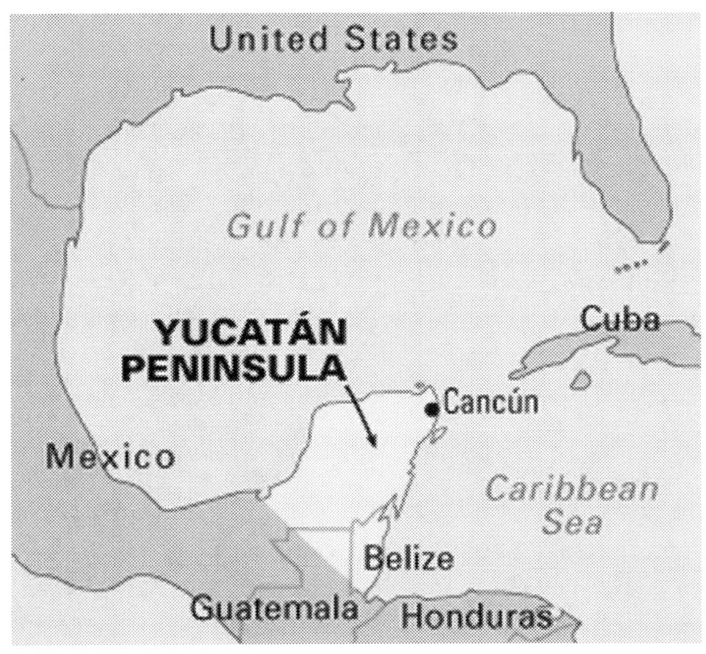

Map of the Gulf of Mexico

As we were nearing Key West, sometime during the night we encountered some bad weather and lost contact with Marcello and the other two guys on the trimaran. When we arrived in Key West, the bad weather followed us in. We barely had time to tie up at the marina, get our sails down, and batten down the hatches before a vicious storm hit.

Once we were safely docked at the municipal pier in Key West, we ran, in heavy rain, into the main building at the Marina. A U.S. Customs officer greeted us. He told us the trimaran had been rescued by a tow out of Miami and that our friends would meet us there. He then asked for our papers.

I showed him my passport and my visa. I fully expected that I was in trouble because of what had happened in Brownsville and what the Consul in Merida had told me. I was expecting the worst.

The man looked at my papers for no more than a few seconds and stamped my passport and visa. I tried not to act surprised and walked away as quickly as possible without saying a word to him. I had made it safely into the U.S. The only thing I could figure was that the government's computers weren't as accurate as I thought they would be, or maybe there were so many people named Jorge Frias they just missed me. Francisco and Alex were completely legal and they had no trouble at all.

For the next week rain and high winds prevented us from leaving port. We spent the days drinking beers at Sloppy Joe's, Margaritaville and the other bars on Duval Street, sleeping on the boat. I called Aunt Elba and told her where I was and to expect me any day. She said Manny was in town and would get me whenever I arrived.

When the weather finally broke, we set sail for Miami. Almost half of our journey was still ahead of us. That first night out of Key West, when the moon was just a sliver of light in the sky, while I was sleeping and Francisco was handling the wheel, he failed to notice a huge tanker coming at us.

Miami is a huge port and there are always dozens, if not hundreds, of cargo ships on the waters off Florida's coast. Those ships are operated by a skeleton crew of sailors and they just stay on one course, expecting everyone to get out of their way. Most have a black hull with only a small red light at the bow and one at the stern and are hard to see even if you are paying close attention.

All of a sudden Francisco starts yelling at us to come quick and when we did we saw the ship, which wasn't far away, heading straight for us, traveling at 20 or 25 knots. The three of us pulled in the sails as fast as we could to change our path and the ship missed us by less than a hundred feet. As it went silently by all we saw was a huge black wall that seemed to be higher than a six story building and longer than a football field. The wake from the ship could have sunk us. If it had hit us, the captain would never have even felt so much as a bump and we would have been left to drown.

Though the wind had died down, the swells from the storm were still very high and the trip was a rough one. On the morning of the fourth day, we came to Government Cut, the inlet that allows boats and ships to cut through from the Atlantic Ocean to Biscayne Bay. It is at the southern tip of Miami Beach. Francisco had a berth reserved at the Key Biscayne Marina and that is where we were headed.

As soon as we entered the Cut, a large U.S. Customs boat with two huge outboard motors on the back came speeding by us. Two young women were on board. I waved at them and they waved back. Alfredo was not happy with me for waving to them and told me not to do that again.

They let us go on our way and didn't stop us. They passed by us two more times and I looked the other way each time. Then, just as we were within eyesight of the marina, they pulled alongside us and started asking questions, being as friendly and as nice as they could be. We told them that we had already cleared customs in Key West but they said we weren't in the U.S. as far as they were concerned. We would have to clear customs again.

I didn't know if that meant Key West wasn't part of the U.S. or if it meant that we were re-entering the U.S. because we had gone back out to sea. Anyone who has been to Key West knows that it is not like anyplace else in the country. They call themselves the "Conch Republic" and pride themselves on being different. Down there, they said if they could secede, they would.

Then the two women told us we would have to go downtown with them. They made us follow them to the pier at the entrance to the

Miami River, which required us to reverse our course and sail an hour back to where we had just come from. They could have pulled us over an hour earlier but for reasons known only to them they waited to do so.

Once we were at the dock, which had U.S. Customs plastered all over it in big, black letters, officers from the D.E.A., Dade County Sheriff's Department, City of Miami Police, Florida Department of Law Enforcement and other U.S. Customs agents, in addition to the two female officers, greeted us. We saw over a dozen police officers in different colored uniforms, some with flak jackets on and all carrying guns. Many had rifles and automatic weapons. It was an impressive display of firepower, and quite intimidating too.

Once we tied up and stepped off the boat the two women told us to sit on the grass. They brought in dogs and proceeded to tear the boat apart. Every now and then the dogs would bark and the two women would yell something to us like, "I think they've found something!" or "What have we here?" All of that was just to make us nervous. Maybe they thought one of us would confess to something when they did that and blame the others, I don't know, but I was worried.

Just days before we left Isla de Mujeres, Francisco had changed the mast. I looked at him and asked, in Spanish, if he had put anything in the new mast. He swore on his mother's life that he hadn't, but the way he said it made me suspicious. I knew that if they found drugs we were going to prison. I was afraid.

Several hours later, an older man drove up in an unmarked car. He stayed in his car but he wasn't parked far from where we were sitting so we could see hear what he was being told and what he was saying in response. He was clearly one of the higher-ups. He looked at our papers and had the others tell him what they were doing. After he'd heard from several people, including the two female officers, we heard him tell them that unless they found drugs on board, and soon, that they had no right to keep us any longer.

After another hour, they let us go, just like that, and we were on our way back towards the marina at Key Biscayne. The boat was a mess. They didn't do anything to even try to fix up what they had torn up. That was our problem.

Francisco had rented an apartment for us at a motel on Biscayne Boulevard, just past the toll booth leading to Key Biscayne, and when we got properly moored at the marina and checked in, we took a taxi to the motel. Marcello and the other two men were there waiting for us, watching television. Marcello was angry with Francisco for leaving him out in the Atlantic and not staying together as they had planned. He said they could have died.

I had to step in between the two men to keep them from fighting. Things were not very pleasant in the apartment so I immediately called my cousin, Manny. I asked him to come get me and he did. We went straight back to Aunt Elba's house in Northwest Miami. I had made it safely into the U.S.

I had no idea why the Customs Agents in either Key West or Miami hadn't discovered anything about what had happened to me at the border in Brownsville. And it wasn't just U.S. Customs. I have to think that the computers for all of the law enforcement agencies involved in that search and seizure operation had put our names in their computers. They didn't even ask me anything about where I was going and what I planned to do either, which surprised me. Maybe they thought that since we were sailors we would just keep on sailing. I had no idea. Maybe I was legal.

Not long after I arrived and before I had settled in, Manny had found me a few jobs to choose from. This time I took a job doing valet parking. The money was better and the work was much easier than in a restaurant. I worked at a place called the Disco Inferno which was at 15th and Washington, right in the heart of South Beach. It was one of the hottest spots in all of South Beach. I met Billy Idol, Aaron Neville and a bunch of stars. I saw a lot of beautiful women too.

I stayed in Miami for seven or eight months. During that time I was pulled over a few times for traffic violations, like running a red light or a stop sign. Again, even though the police officers put my name in the computer they always let me go. I figured they maybe had more important things to worry about, like drug smugglers, robbers, rapists and people like that. I didn't know but I kept thinking that maybe I wasn't on their radar screen anymore. Maybe I was legally in the country after all, except for the working part.

While working as a valet driver, my friendship with Matt Sky continued to develop. He was the first gringo that I befriended, as I recall. If not the first, he was the one with whom I developed the best friendship. As a general rule, I steered clear of getting too close to Americans as I figured that the less people knew about me the better, especially Americans.

The Atlantic borders Miami to the east. To the north lay Ft. Lauderdale, the Palm Beaches, Delray and a line of cities all the way up to Jacksonville. To the south was the Conch Republic. To the west was the Everglades, a wilderness area full of alligators, snakes, bugs and other wildlife.

That winter, Matt and I and several of our friends went on several camping trips into the Everglades. We couldn't do that during the summer months because the mosquitoes would eat us alive, but in the winter, South Florida and the Everglades is a great place. Even though Miami was no hotter than Progreso or Cancun in the summer, I never spent a single summer in Miami. I always went north.

On those camping trips, we spent many nights in tents deep in the Everglades. We saw alligators, many beautiful birds and plenty of fish. Matt was like me, a person who loved the outdoors and adventure. He was an excellent fisherman too, and had fished in Alaska one summer. We became good friends, the best friend I ever had in the States, especially for a gringo. He taught me all about the Everglades on those trips. I told him that if he ever came to visit Mexico that I would show him the sights of the Yucatan.

That spring, which was the spring of 1993, although things were going fairly well for me in Miami, and even though I knew that if I left the United States I might not be able to get back, when an opportunity presented itself I decided to go back to Progreso to see my family and be on the water again.

Francisco asked me to accompany him on a 42 foot Binitou sailboat from Miami to Cancun. I was to be a crew mate and get paid for helping him deliver the boat for a man from Switzerland. He knew that I would be a good helper for him on the trip as I had sailed with him before. He was to be the captain, even though the owner of the boat would be sailing with us. I would be allowed to do much of the sailing too, which appealed to me. I agreed to go.

The boat was almost brand new and it sailed magnificently. We made it back to Cancun in three days because of a strong tailwind. When I got to Cancun the owner was happy with the way I performed and wanted to hire me to work with Alex and operate the boat for people who would charter it from him. He would make his money from arranging the charters and handling the business side of things. We were to be paid well for doing the work of sailing the boat.

Just as we were shaking hands and I was telling him that I would accept the job, I turned and saw Matthew Sky and my cousin, Manny, standing there less than twenty feet away, waving to me. I had to turn the job down. I had told Matthew that if he ever made it to Mexico I would show him around and I had to keep my promise.

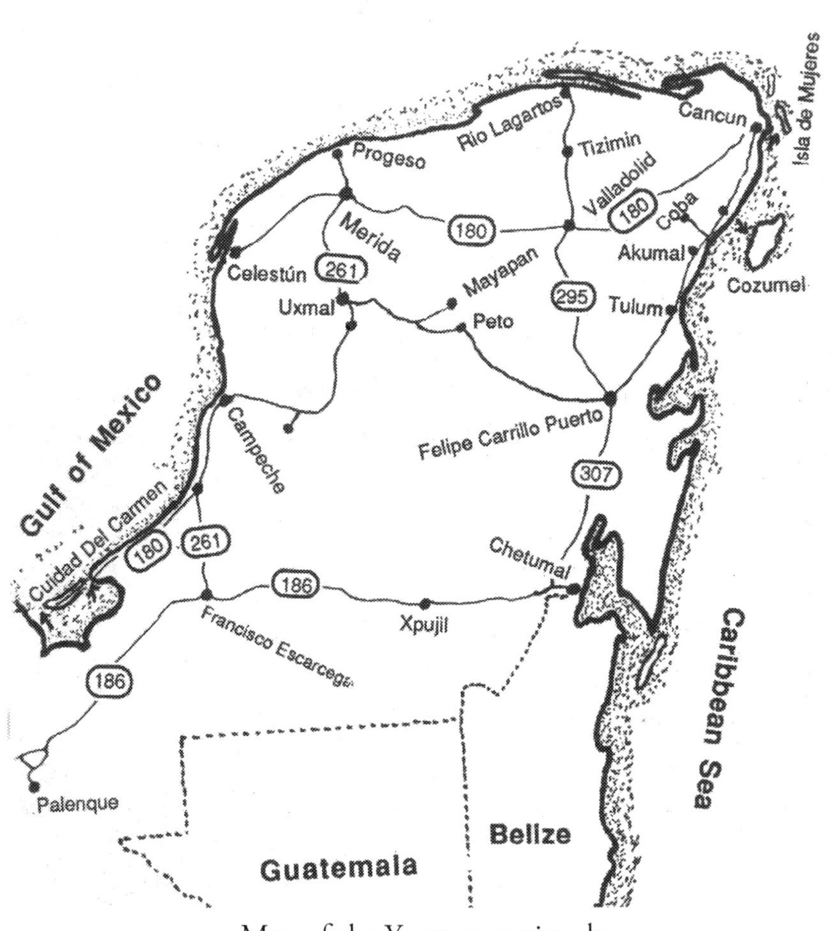

Map of the Yucatan peninsula

Chapter Five

Exploring the Yucatan Peninsula

Their plan was to tour the entire Yucatan Peninsula, including going south into Belize and Guatemala, which are considered to be a part of the Yucatan. I was to show Matthew and Manny all about the Mayans and our culture. The Yucatan Peninsula juts out into the Gulf of Mexico and the Caribbean Sea like a big thumb from the coast line of Mexico. Cancun is the furthest point to the east at the very tip of that thumb.

We left right then and there from the dock in Cancun in the car Matthew had rented. They had been waiting a few days for me to arrive and were ready to go once I got there. We headed south towards Chetumal, which is the southernmost point in Mexico on the Caribbean side. It is the last city in Mexico and we planned to cross the border there on our way into Belize and Guatemala. Our plan was that after visiting those two countries we would come back into Mexico, go through Palenque and then on to Campeche, which is a port city on the other side of the Yucatan, on the Gulf of Mexico side.

From there, we would go to my home town of Progreso, which is on the tip of the thumb on the other side of the Yucatan Peninsula from Cancun. Matthew was to fly out of Cancun back to the United States in two months. We were going to stop at as many of the temples and ruins as we could along the way. We planned to take our time and enjoy ourselves. We had no schedule and were not in a hurry.

Matthew had rented the smallest and cheapest car he could find. It had power steering and an air-conditioner but that was about it. There were many temples and sights I had heard of but never seen before either and I was looking forward to the journey just as much as they were. Manny had grown up in Chicago and although his parents were Mexicans and from the Yucatan he didn't know too much more than Matt. Though he had dual citizenship, he was mostly an American.

Since we had little money, we planned to camp out most of the time and eat the fish we caught as often as possible. We had only one tent between the three of us. We weren't planning to stay at any commercial places along the way other than to shower when absolutely necessary. It wasn't like the United States in that respect. You go anywhere in the U.S. and you will find national parks, state parks, county parks and thousands of private campgrounds, like KOAs, with electricity, showers and modern facilities. Not so in the Yucatan. There were some primitive campgrounds, but few had any electricity or running water.

The first place we went was to Tulum, since it was the closest. We arrived at Tulum an hour after leaving Cancun. It is built right on the coast line. The very first Conquistadores who sailed along the east coast of the Yucatan back in the early 1600s reported seeing great stone structures as grand as anything they had seen in Europe. It is widely believed that those men had seen Tulum.

We arrived at Tulum late that morning and I showed Matthew and Manny all around the city, which has been beautifully restored. Tulum is a walled city situated on the edge of a cliff overlooking the Caribbean. It was called the "City of the Dawn" by the Mayans, probably because it saw the sun rise every morning. No other Mayan city was so situated. The cliffs are 40 feet above the water. It is said to be the most visited archeological site in the Mayan world, even more so than Chichen-Itza or Tikal, which is the biggest and possibly the oldest Mayan site. Tikal has the highest of temples and over 3000 historical sites have been uncovered there so far. It encompasses forty eight square miles, the approximate size of San Francisco. It is in Guatemala and I was looking forward to seeing it because that is one of the temples I had never been to.

Tulum was magnificent and, due to the heavy volume of tourists who visit it, much money has been spent making it as good as can be. Its proximity to Cancun and Playa del Carmen is undoubtedly the reason why so many people go there instead of Tikal or Chichen-Itza.

What is most unusual about Tulum is that, unlike virtually every other Mayan city, it remained inhabited up to the time the Spaniards first set foot on Yucatan soil in 1511. Within 50 years after the Spaniards arrived it was deserted and it remained deserted for centuries, although Pirates took up home in its coves for a while during the late seventeenth and early eighteenth centuries.

The most impressive site on the grounds is El Castillo, or "The Castle," which sits high above the other buildings. The intellect of the Mayan people remains evident to this day at Tulum inside the Castle. The fact that the structures have endured for almost two thousand years is remarkable but their ingenuity is remarkable as well.

At the top of El Castillo, the Mayans placed lanterns which showed sailors the way into and out of the harbor at night. Even now, if two candles were placed on the shelves at the top of the structure in the intended way the beams of light cast by those lanterns meet out in the Caribbean Sea, and where the beams cross marks the channel for ships to enter the harbor. It provides a beacon for ships to enter even now.

A cenote

A great wall, fifteen to twenty feet high, stretching over two-thirds of a mile long, encloses the city. Five gateways allow entrance, with a toll at each. As with all of the other Mayan temples, there was a cenote, or spring-fed pond, inside the walls of the city.

In 1517 another Spaniard, Juan de Grijalva, sailed by Tulum and said, "We travelled by a city so large that Seville seemed to us neither larger nor better." It was at Tulum that Gonzalo Guerrero led Mayan warriors against his former countrymen and defeated the Spanish army. He is said to have relied upon ambushes and the element of surprise. The term guerilla warfare supposedly came into being as a result of his tactics.

Tulum was connected to Coba and Chichen-Itza and other Mayan areas by great roads made of stone. Not even the Romans or the Greeks, or any other known civilization up to the late twentieth century, had anything to compare to the roads and the infrastructure developed by the Mayans. We walked through the city in a few hours time. By early afternoon Matthew and Manny were ready to move on. They had seen enough. They weren't tourists, they were adventurers. They wanted action.

After visiting Tulum, we headed for Coba, which was about a half hour drive to the northeast on a pothole-filled road through the jungle. Coba is sometimes called the "lost" city because, although a man named Thompson did some preliminary work there in the early 1900s, it wasn't until 1973 that excavations began. It is estimated that the city, which once held over 50,000 people, had been deserted for a thousand years.

Five or more lakes surround the area. Legend has it that there were well-constructed roads leading out of Coba in fifty different directions, the longest of which was 62 miles and led all the way to Chichen-Itza. Coba was supposedly the hub for the entire area. It is best known for its pyramid-like temples, one of which is 138 feet tall and is the largest and highest in northern Yucatan.

It was late in the day by the time we left Coba. We wanted to get our camp set up before the sun went down. We found a spot off the road with no sign of civilization anywhere around. It had been early morning when I arrived in Cancun and after being in the sailboat for several days I was in need of a shower. I needed to wash my clothes, too. Both would have to wait.

We found a spot so that our tent and our car couldn't be seen from the road but the site we chose wasn't near any water. There wasn't much desirable about the spot we picked at all except for the price and its remoteness. Matthew was looking for an adventure and he was going to get it.

Although I had traveled the area for years, I had never spent a night in the jungle in as remote an area as we were in. The first thing we did was gather wood for a fire, which wasn't an easy thing to do. The jungle wasn't like a forest where we could find downed branches from trees which would easily burn. Most of what we found was mostly green or had dissolved to the point where it wouldn't burn. It was a major accomplishment for us to get the fire going and keep it going. None of us had a gun, other than a spear gun, and the only real weapon we had was a long knife.

That first night in the jungle was something neither Matthew, Manny of I had ever experienced. Our camping trips to the Everglades, or Matthew's trips out west in Alaska or Montana couldn't hold a candle to it. The Yucatan is home to more howler monkeys than anyplace else in the world. The howlers are large animals and are said to be among the largest monkeys in the world. They range from 56 to 92 centimeters, not counting their tail, which can be as long as their bodies are. They have a prehensile tail, which means the tail is adapted to be able to grasp and/or hold onto the limb of a tree while the monkey feeds and uses his hands and feet to do other things.

Howler monkeys rarely leave the trees. They feed at the canopy of trees and are usually found at the tops of the largest trees. They aren't particularly active and don't move very fast. They avoid any contact with humans or other animals and stay together in large groups. They don't do well in captivity and, in fact, there are no howler monkeys to be found at any zoos in the world. They are not anybody's pet either.

At night they howl, hence their names, and the sounds they make will frighten anyone and everyone. Although they are rarely aggressive, their howl, which is a low, loud, guttural sound, much like the sound an agitated gorilla or orangutan makes, is terrifying. They howled the entire night. I don't know if Matthew or Manny got any sleep, but I didn't, even though I knew there was little chance they would attack us.

There are also spider monkeys in the area, as well as in other parts of Central and South America. Spider monkeys are even longer, though not as big, as the howler monkeys. They make the noises most people usually associate with monkeys found at zoos, not like the howlers, and they travel more. Because they are large, both the howler monkeys and the spider monkeys are hunted for their meat by the natives. We heard the screeches of the spider monkeys that night too, and even though we knew that they weren't going to bother us, the noises scared us or, at the very least, made it difficult to sleep.

The largest population of jaguars on the planet is on the Yucatan Peninsula. The jaguars were gods to the ancient Maya. Drawings of jaguars are found on frescos at many of the most ancient of temples. The jaguar was and still is a dangerous carnivore and it, more than any other creature in the jungle, was likely to attack us if we happened to be in its way, or so we thought. There were pumas and ocelots too, but the jaguar is the biggest and baddest cat in those jungles. Jaguars don't usually attack humans, unless provoked or threatened in some way, and we knew that, but we were still apprehensive of a jaguar being anywhere in the vicinity.

The most dangerous creature to worry about was, without a doubt, the bushmaster, or lachesis, the most venomous of pit vipers in Central and South America. They are known to reach twelve feet in length, though usually they are between six and a half to eight and a half feet long. They are like a rattle snake without rattles, so you can't hear them when they're coming towards you.

I have heard it said that if a person is bitten by a bushmaster he is dead within minutes. Now if there were any bushmasters around, we were in trouble, but since they make no sounds, we wouldn't know it until after we were bitten and then it was too late. Some people called them the "seven-step" killers because if you were bitten you would be dead before you took seven steps.

We saw many people in that part of the country who were missing an arm or a leg and we wondered why that was. We were told that they probably had been bitten by the bushmaster and they had cut the limb off themselves, knowing that if they didn't, they would have died.

Of course, the things that actually caused us the most problems were the smaller creatures…the bugs and the biting insects, like mosquitoes and 'no-see-ums,' called "chicistas." The smoke from the fire kept them away, but that meant that we had to be near the fire and the smoke for it to do us any good.

Fortunately, we made it through the night but after that night we swore that we would "go coastal" and stay on the water the rest of the way as much as possible. If we couldn't be on the coast, we planned to be near the water, whether that was a lake or a cenote.

Historically, one of the main problems for the inhabitants of the Yucatan was the lack of water. There were no major rivers in the Yucatan. One of the theories as to why the Mayans left their temples and abandoned the magnificent cities they had built was that they lacked sufficient water and it prevented them from irrigating their crops properly and providing enough water for the inhabitants, too. Their primary crop was maize, or corn. All of the cities were built in close proximity to a cenote but there may have come a time when that was not enough. Who knows why the Mayan civilization mysteriously disappeared? No one.

After spending the night in the jungle, getting eaten by bugs and mosquitoes, we decided to head straight for the coast without delay. We went to a place called Sian Ka'an, which was about two hours away. It is on the Caribbean Sea and it is an extremely large barrier reef, second largest in the world. Only the Great Barrier Reef in Australia is larger. It extends from the tip of the coast of the Yucatan near Cancun in Mexico southwards past Belize and on into Honduras.

Sian Ka'an lies in the state of Quintana Roo, one of the three Mexican states in the Yucatan Peninsula, Campeche and the Yucatan being the other two states. It had become a sanctuary in 1986 when UNESCO, a world-wide organization whose primary purpose is to preserve for the entire world unique eco-systems and natural marvels. They chose Sian Ka'an to be one of those World Heritage Sites. It is approximately 1.3 million acres in size and spans almost a third of the Caribbean coast of Mexico.

The name Sian Ka'an comes from the Mayans and means "where the sky is born." There are five entrances to Sian Ka'an and we went in through Chac Mool. Guards greeted us and took down our information, but camping is permitted so they welcomed us to the sanctuary. There was no campground area, though, and we were told that we could camp wherever we wanted, except on top of a dune or in any of the sensitive areas.

Sian Ka'an is a diverse ecosystem all unto itself. There are great white beaches with large coastal dunes. There are also marshlands, mangroves, savannas and swamps, all part of wetlands that provide a buffer between the Ocean and the land. In addition to the waters of the Caribbean Sea, there are also fresh water lagoons and cenotes too. The brackish lagoons have fresh water in them and where those lagoons of fresh water meet the salt water from the ocean many diverse creatures converge. For example, two distinct species of crocodile, not usually found together, inhabit the area.

After we checked in and gave them the license plate number to our vehicle, and some personal information, we never saw anyone again until we drove out two weeks later. We went looking for a cenote, which is basically an opening where the limestone rock, which is the bedrock of the land mass in the Yucatan, has weakened and given way. There are aquifers running below the land throughout all of the Yucatan and they connect cenotes.

The Mayans believed that when people died they went to the underworld. They believed that the rulers of the underworld lived in the waters inside cenotes. They were considered to be sacred places. We made camp behind a dune, not far from the ocean or from a fresh water lagoon, right next to the largest cenote we were able to find.

We immediately started a fire and then went for a swim in the ocean. We found lobster in shallow waters not far from the beach and Matthew was able to spear some grouper and a hogfish. Manny used a cast-net and caught some mullet. We had a feast that night and the bugs weren't anywhere near as bad as they had been the night before.

Since we were on the coast the wind off the water helped to drive the bugs and mosquitoes away. The smoke from the fire helped too. We stayed there for two full weeks, swimming, fishing and eating. It was a magical spot. We never saw any sign of another human being except for some boats which were far off-shore.

I can't say that we tired of the place, because it was like being Robinson Crusoe in the book by Daniel Defoe or like being Tom Hanks in the movie Castaway, but Matthew and Manny had other places they wanted to see, so when we left Sian Ka'an, we headed south towards Chetumal.

Chetumal is only a few hundred miles from Cancun but it is separated by centuries. It is said that Gonzalo Gerrero was taken as a slave in 1511 to the Mayan city of Ichpaatan at the north of the Bay of Chetumal. The first mestizo was born when Gonzalo fathered a child by a Mayan princess, Zazal Ha, to whom he was married. His oldest child was a girl, Ixmo, the first Mestizo of Mexico.

Chetumal was the site of many battles between the natives and the English, Spanish, pirates and others for centuries. It wasn't until 1930 when its name was changed from Payo Obispo to Chetumal that some sense of permanency evolved. It was, once and for all, finally recognized as being a part of Mexico.

Because we left so late in the day we ended up driving in the dark towards Chetumal. We planned on renting a room at a motel and enjoying long, hot showers. We were the only ones on what was a deserted road, one lane in each direction. Matthew was driving. Manny and I were asleep.

Matthew saw a sign that said "ALTO." Later, he told us that he was puzzled by it because he wondered why there would be a sign on the road saying "HIGH," which is a correct translation of the word, but the word also means "STOP." When he blew by it at whatever speed he was going, which was above the speed limit, I'm sure, he heard whistles. When he looked over, he saw a small wooden building along the side of the road and two men, who weren't in any uniforms, standing outside the gatehouse. He saw that one of the men was pointing an M-16 in his direction, motioning him to stop. That is when he yelled to us to wake up. He turned the vehicle around and drove back to the guard house.

The two men told us to get out of the car and asked to see our identification papers. Since they didn't have any uniforms on, and I couldn't tell who they were, I asked them who they were and what authority they had to stop us. I was as Mexican as they were and I wasn't afraid to speak my mind. The one guy looks over at the other guy holding the rifle and says, "The man wants to know what authority we have, Pedro. Show him."

At that, the man points his rifle at me, chambers a round, and says, "Any other questions, cabron?" Matthew whispered to me telling me to shut up and do whatever they said. Later he told me that he was sure they were going to just shoot us and leave us to rot. No one would ever have known.

The man with the gun told us to sit on a bench next to what was an 8 foot by 8 foot wooden shack. He kept an eye on us, with a hand on his rifle at all times, while the other began searching the car. Shortly after, a car pulled up and another man got out. He was obviously the "jefe" or the chief of the three. He was dressed to the hilt and was clearly a Federale.

We all noticed that the fingernail on his right pinky finger was at least an inch longer than the rest of his fingernails. He took over searching the vehicle and started with my bag. We noticed how he would pull things out of the car using the elongated fingernail.

Both Manny and Matthew had some weed on them and they were sure the man would find it. I didn't have any in my bag because Francisco wouldn't allow it on board for fear that his boat would be seized and taken from him, which would have happened if the U.S. Coast Guard had found any narcotics aboard on a routine search.

When the man came upon my dirty underwear, which was still wet and hadn't been washed from my sailing voyage, he pulled out the dirtiest and nastiest of all. When he did, after not finding any drugs up to that point, as soon as he got a whiff of what that underwear smelled like, he dropped it on the driver's seat, backed away from the car and told us to get up and get out of there. He had a look of complete disgust as he did. We wasted no time doing what we had been told to do.

We laughed and laughed for days about how my dirty laundry saved our asses, which it did. Those guys were scary and there was nobody anywhere close to where we were and nobody else on the road at that time of night who could have stopped them from doing whatever they wanted to do. I drove the rest of the way, making sure that we stayed below the speed limit and didn't violate any laws.

Because Chetumal is a border town it has a strong military presence even though there hadn't been any fighting between the countries in the area in many years. It is comprised of a wide variety of cultures, including freed African slaves, Chinese, Koreans and people from the Middle East, as well as a high percentage of indigenous peoples and Mestizos. It's a city of several hundred thousand people and we had no problem finding a cheap motel. We all took long showers that night. We were so tired that we didn't even go out for dinner or for beers. We all enjoyed sleeping in a bed for a change.

We got up early the next morning, had some breakfast, washed our clothes, cleaned up the car as best we could, and started to wander about Chetumal. A large fence separates Mexico from Belize and we happened to walk by one of the places where cars passed through customs on their way either to or from Mexico. Soon after we did, we found out that we had a serious problem.

Guards were on both sides of the border and we saw that people had to clear customs on both sides. I spoke to one of the Mexican guards and he told me that the Mexican government wouldn't allow us to take the rental car out of the country. We knew that on the rental contract we had indicated that we had no plans to leave the country but we didn't think the border guards would care about that. We were going to have to change plans.

Also, there was an uprising of some sort going on in that part of Mexico at the time. The farmers were unhappy about something and had threatened a strike. There were hundreds more Federales and police on the streets than usual and we could sense the tension.

Matthew might have been the only gringo in the whole town, I think, and at 6'4" tall he stood out in the crowd. He felt like everyone was looking at him and no one was liking what they saw. He didn't like the city at all and wanted to leave right away but we stayed a second night at the motel, went out for a good dinner and an even better night of drinking. We left the following day. We were ready to get back into the jungle.

Matthew wanted to go to Palenque, which is another of the hundreds of ancient Mayan temples, but it is located high in the mountains in the center of the Yucatan. I told Matthew that was not a good place to go at the time because it wasn't a safe place to be. I didn't want to go there, but he didn't believe me so, against my better judgment and against my advice, we headed for Palenque.

Palenque is in the Tumbala Mountains in the middle of what is a rain forest. It lay hidden for more than eight centuries after it was abandoned by the Maya in the ninth century. I had heard that the ruins are as compelling and as beautiful as any of the others.

I think Matthew wanted to go to Palenque mostly because he had seen it in the first Star Wars movie. The rebels had used it as their base of operations and that was how he heard of it. He wouldn't admit it, but that's what I thought.

Whenever we found signs for a Mayan ruin we drove to it. Most of the time there was a small sign along the side of the road saying that a Mayan temple was in the neighborhood and more often than not we drove down a dirt road to get to it. We never knew what we would find.

On our way to Palenque we came across this one site which had not been developed or improved at all. I don't remember if it had a name or not. We saw the sign and turned off to go see it.

Grass, bushes and other forces of nature had overtaken the stones which once had been temples, houses, and who knows what else. We were looking at all of the buildings, as we usually did, trying to find iguanas, which were called the guardians of the temples, and we almost always found some at every temple, usually dozens of them. It was rare that anyone else was there with us. We usually had the places to ourselves, especially the remote spots.

This time, though, the three of us were standing on top of a flat surface which had been the floor of what seemed to be a fortification of some kind. There was a wall still standing and we could envision ourselves standing behind the wall and defending it against armed invaders. As we were standing there that day we saw five or six guys coming towards us, all of whom were carrying guns.

Maybe they were hunters, maybe they were rebels, maybe they were robbers, maybe they were Federales...we didn't know and we didn't care. We all ducked down, stopped talking, slowly and silently crept back the way we came, using hand signals, and when we thought we were out of sight, behind the ruin enough so they couldn't see us, we ran as fast as we could back to the car and sped away. I screamed at Matthew, saying that I had told him that there were armed rebels in the area and that we shouldn't go to Palenque. After seeing the armed men, he agreed not to go to Palenque.

That only happened to us that one time. Most of the time we had no trouble at all. Some days we took hikes off the road on dirt trails, or beaten paths, not knowing where we were going or what we might find. One thing I did before we left Chetumal was to buy a large bag of candy. Neither Matthew nor Manny knew why and I said something like, "you'll see."

Whenever we went on hikes into the jungle to see ruins, get to a cenote, or just see what we would find, we would often come upon a village that was nothing more than a few straw huts with a circle of fire in the middle. That happened to us at least a dozen times. We usually came through during the day and when we did most of the time we found only young children in the village. Many times the children had no clothes on. There might be a teenager watching them, but basically they were watching themselves. These people probably had no Spanish blood in them whatsoever and were true Indios, or indigenous MesoAmericans, who could not even be called Mexicans since they were there long before Mexico came into existence as a country.

At first, they would eye us very suspiciously, but when we gave them candy they immediately loved us because of it. It seemed as if some of them had never seen candy before in their lives. The adults must have been out hunting or gathering food for dinner. When any adults were around, they liked us for giving candy to the children and making them smile. We never had any trouble with the native people, the ones who lived in the jungle who undoubtedly had little contact with the outside world other than the occasional wanderers like us. Maybe it was because of the candy and maybe it was because they were basically friendly people, not wanting any trouble. I didn't know but the candy worked like magic.

After that experience we had on the way to Palenque, we turned around and headed back towards Chetumal. Not far from Chetumal was Mexico's largest cenote, called Cenote Azul, or the Blue Spring. We took a little detour and had to back-track to get to it. It was several hours out of our way but it was worth it.

We jumped into the water as soon as we got there and spent the rest of the day swimming. At sunset, we decided to splurge and have dinner at the restaurant located on the rim of the cenote. We rarely went to a restaurant to eat during the entire two months we were there but we ate there that night because it was such a beautiful atmosphere.

The cenote is 300 feet deep and has a 600 foot diameter. The water was crystal clear and we could see the many people diving down deep into the waters below us while we swimming on top. Because the water was so clear we could easily see the bottom, too, but that was deceptive because it was much deeper than it looked. It is the supposedly the largest and the deepest cenote in the Yucatan. There is a fort not far from there called San Felipe but we didn't go there. We camped a few miles away, in the jungle, and swam there for several days.

The second day we were there, swimming and diving in the Cenote Azul, Matthew did a stupid thing. He had put the keys to the vehicle in his shorts that he was swimming in. As could be expected, he lost the keys. We had to call for a locksmith to come make us a new set of keys, but he had to come to where we were camped to do that, and since we were camped in the jungle and that was where the car was, he had to get through the jungle to get to the car to make the key. We were fairly deep in the jungle, down a dirt path, way off the main road.

It took two days for the locksmith to get there, once he found out where the car was, and when he did he arrived on horseback with a buddy. While the guy was making us a new key, the other guy was riding the horse all around. He let us ride the horse too. They made us a new key and it worked fine, but that wasn't something that I would ever have seen in the United States. It was completely unbelievable to Matthew and Manny, too. That was just another of the many, many differences between life in Mexico and life in the United States, and it was comical.

When the key was finally made and delivered we decided to leave, even though it was late in the afternoon. We planned to stay at another cenote near the Mayan city of Calakmul. It was discovered from the air by a biologist named Cyrus Lundell in 1931. In Mayan, 'ca' means 'two', 'lak' means 'adjacent', and 'mul' signifies any artificial mound or pyramid. So the name 'Calakmul' means the 'City of the Two Adjacent Pyramids'."

Calakmul was a major Mayan community within the Yucatan a couple of thousand plus years ago. It is one of the oldest known Mayan communities. Tikal in Guatemala and Calakmul were said to be the two most powerful cities at one time. Calakmul supposedly had a population of over 50,000 people at the height of its power.

Almost 7,000 ancient structures have been located and restoration of many of the buildings has been completed. The largest of the restored structures is the great pyramid. It is 55 meters high, making it the tallest known Mayan pyramid, at least as far as what we were told. Four tombs had been located within the pyramid so it was like what the Egyptians did in that respect. We walked around and saw as much as we could see, but then went to find a cenote to swim in and a place to camp.

The thing we were most interested in about Calakmul was that it was supposed to be a great place to see Toucans. Matthew wanted to see some and we went looking for them. They are a very common bird in the Yucatan, though they are somewhat hard to find.

The Keel-billed Toucan, sometimes called the Rainbow-billed Toucan, is a colorful bird with a large bill. It is the national bird of Belize. Measuring from the tip of its bill, the Keel-billed Toucans are usually somewhere around 17 to 22 inches long Their bills are about 5 to 6 inches long, which is almost a third of its total length. They have a black body with a yellow neck and chest and their bills are usually green with a red tip and orange sides. It has blue feet and red feathers at the tip of its tail.

One unusual feature about it is that its toes face in different directions. It has two toes facing forward and two facing back. Because the Toucans spend a large portion of time in the trees, at the very tops of the trees, this helps them to stay on the branches of the trees with no trouble. They make a loud, rasping sound, and are usually found in groups. We saw some, but only from a distance.

We didn't stay there too long because Matthew got a little impatient after not being able to find any more than a few Toucans after two days of searching for them. We decided to get back on the road and head to Campeche. Matthew didn't have too many days left before he would fly back to the U.S. and Manny and I wanted to make sure he had enough time to spend in Progreso with our family. Manny's brother, Gabriel, was there and we all wanted to see him, so we headed for Campeche.

Matthew was 23 and Manny was a year older. I was the oldest at 30. I had forgotten all about Rayna, Mary, getting back to the U.S., playing soccer, making money, doing tours and everything else during those two months. We were having a good time being explorers. I had never taken so much time off to do what I was doing in my life. Whatever Matthew and Manny wanted to do was fine with me.

On the way to Campeche, we found a sign for a cave. We hadn't explored any caves up to that point and Matthew wanted to go in so we did. The caves are dried-up cenotes. They occur when a sinkhole with rocks surrounding it, holding in groundwater, collapses. Way down into the caves there is usually some water, since there is an aquifer connecting all the cenotes, but sometimes you have to go far to get to it. We came to this one place and the sign said "Mayan ruin" or something like that.

There was an old guy sitting in a chair next to a wooden shack on a dirt road. No one else was around. There was a patch of dirt behind the shack. We parked the car and went to talk to the man.

The ancient Mayans regarded caves as entrances into the underworld. Some of their most sacred rituals were performed far underground. An iron gate blocked our path to where the cave was located. The man told us that there was a dried-up cenote and some Mayan artifacts inside the cave. We gave him about six pesos, or fifty cents, and he pointed us in the direction of a dirt path. There was no map or informational flyer or even a sheet of paper. We had no idea what we were in for.

We walked down into the cave, single file, on a small, narrow path. There were no light bulbs to light the way. We were soon in darkness, using flashlights to see. I didn't even have a flashlight. Matthew and Manny each had one, so I walked in the middle, between the two of them. I couldn't see much at all.

Several times Manny and I wanted to turn around but Matthew wanted to go on. We followed the path deeper and deeper inside the cave. There was water down there and he was determined to find it and swim in it.

Matthew saved my life that day. I was walking a little too fast in the darkness of the cave and I almost stepped off the path, which was a cliff, that for sure would have hurt me very badly at the very least and probably killed me. I lost my balance and was falling and he grabbed me and pulled me back. I really don't know how far I would have fallen, but I do know that it would have been a long way. We kept going, but I was more careful.

We walked as far as we could, climbing down the rocks and crawling on the ground. At times that ground was moist and movable. We later found out that it was bat shit. We saw stalactites coming out of the ceiling and slagmites too. Matthew's determination was worth it as we eventually came to what was a large canyon type area with a large cenote in the middle.

Jorge at the entrance to a cave.

We came to a spot where we couldn't go any further unless we climbed down a rope ladder. I didn't want to go any further, but Matthew did. He started down the ladder and even though a couple of the wooden parts broke as he went he kept going. At the bottom, we were able to see a statue of "Chac," the god of rain, sitting on an island in the middle of the cenote. There were stone altars and other relics from the past. We swam in the water and were immediately refreshed for the journey back. It was very unusual to look up and see the roots of trees above us, but that is what we saw that day.

When we got back to the top, we were glad we went, but I remember thinking that was another example of how much different things are in the U.S. from what they are like in Mexico. I never, ever, went to a park in the United States where there were no rangers or where there were dangerous conditions like what we found at any number of places, but that cave was probably the worst. If Matthew hadn't caught me when I had slipped, or if Matthew had lost his grip on the rope swing, or if we had fallen off the path at any number of places, we were dead. On the way back, we dropped rocks down into the darkness to see how far down it went and it seemed like it went down for at least a couple of hundred feet. The whole trip was like that, one adventure after another.

We arrived in Campeche the next day. It was founded in 1540, two years before Merida was founded, by the Spanish conquistador, Francisco Montejo, and it is on the shore of the Bay of Campeche in the Gulf of Mexico. It now has a population of slightly over 200,000 people. It was built over or on top of the Mayan city of Kimpech, or Canpech. In Mayan, that meant "lord of the serpent tick."

There were supposedly 3000 houses and monuments at one time in the Mayan city before it was, like all of the others, abandoned during the middle of the tenth century. None of the Mayan temples and buildings remain any more. The stones from the temples and structures were used to build the Spanish houses and buildings.

The city was attacked many times by pirates and buccaneers over a period of time spanning at least 160 years during the 17th and 18th centuries. Because of the frequent invasions, the Spanish built a wall around the city, with guns and fortifications to protect themselves from the attacks. The wall still exists.

There are over a thousand Spanish buildings in Campeche now

protected as historical by UNESCO as a World Heritage Site. There are four gates which allow access to the walled city, which was over two miles in total length, shaped like a hexagon. Back in the day only the Spanish were allowed inside the walls. The native Mayans and indigenous peoples lived outside the walls in what was called the barrios.

We didn't spend much time there. We weren't interested in being tourists and had seen enough of Spanish forts and things but we did wander through the walled portion of the city for a few hours. We spent most of the day getting cleaned up, washing our clothes, taking long, hot showers and getting a good, hot meal. We lay on our beds and enjoyed the air-conditioned room. By the next day, after a good night of drinking and having fun, we were ready to get back in the jungle. Matthew and Manny were ready for more adventure.

Before we left Campeche, however, Matthew had another encounter with Mexican law enforcement authorities. This time it was the local police, not the Federales as before. Matthew was driving and I think Manny may have been sleeping in the back. I wasn't paying attention, but the next thing I knew he was cursing and bringing the car to a stop.

A police officer was walking towards us. Matthew said that the police man, who was directing traffic at a large roundabout intersection, had motioned for him to go, and when he did, the officer must have noticed that he was a gringo and started blowing his whistle, directing him to stop.

I didn't see what happened, so I didn't say anything. I just listened. The officer said Matthew had disobeyed his instructions. Matthew said as politely as he could in broken Spanish that he saw the man had motioned for him to go. The officer disagreed and said that he would have to give him a ticket. The officer said it would cost 150 pesos, or about $18.

Matthew didn't want to pay it, saying he was innocent. The officer said that if Matthew would give him the 150 pesos, he would take care of the matter for him. Matthew said that he wanted to get the ticket and that he would like to fight it in court. Of course, I knew that Matthew had no intention of staying to appear in court but I also knew that the officer wasn't going to let him go without getting any money. It was, as they say, a "Mexican stand-off."

When it became obvious that neither man was backing down, Manny and I got out of the car and walked away from the car with the officer, outside of Matthew's hearing, to talk it over with him. We gave him 50 pesos, or $6.00, and he let us go. Matthew was angry about it, saying that it wasn't fair. I told him that's the way things were in Mexico. The police don't get paid much and they supplement their income by taking money from traffic violators, never intending to turn the money in.

Everyone knew that and everyone accepted it, even though it wasn't right. Most people were expected to thank the police officer for handling the matter for them so that they didn't have to appear in court. Of course, most people might have been guilty of the offense, but maybe not. Matthew swore up and down that he was innocent and that something like that would never happen in the United States.

Although I had read about crooked cops in the U.S., and I'm sure there are some, most of the ones I knew and had met were honest and played by the rules. In Mexico, I think most people, including me, would tell you that most of the police were not honest and that they all looked for an opportunity to make a little extra money any time they had a chance to do so. Matthew swore he was never going back.

From there, we headed towards Chichen-Itza. Of all the Mayan ruins, that was the one Matthew wanted to see the most. It was the one he had heard of more than any of the others. That was the one he had seen pictures of. That was the one he had to see before he left to go back to the States.

He told me that before he came down to Mexico he had called his old boss out at Yosemite National Park in California and had a job waiting for him as a guide for the trail rides on horses through the park once the summer season started. He only had a couple of weeks left before he had to start work there.

On the way to Chichen-Itza, we stopped at the Balankanche Cave, which we came to a few miles before we got to Chichen Itza. It was a famous site and it had been well-restored, not like the last one we had been in. Balankanche Cave was supposed to be a ceremonial site for the Aztecs, not the Mayans, but it could have been a Mayan site before then. I didn't know and it didn't say.

A local tour guide discovered the cave in 1959 when, by accident, he stumbled upon a passageway leading to a deep cavern. He supposedly went two hours down the dark path, by himself. He found treasures left by the ancient Aztecs hundreds of years before.

We went in and saw hundreds of stalactites surrounding a huge stalagmite which went from floor to the ceiling in the middle of a huge area. It looked like a Ceiba tree. Both the Aztecs and the Mayans thought of the Ceiba tree as a "sacred tree inside the earth." All of whatever it was the guide found was gone, except for the stalactites and stalagmites. It was a temple to the Aztec rain god, named Tlaloc.

After leaving Balankanche we went to Chichen-Itza. It is by far the best restored site in all of the Yucatan, except possibly Tulum, though it is much bigger and much more impressive than Tulum is. In 1890, an American meat magnate, Allison Armour, bought Chichen-Itza and 100 acres surrounding it for $75, supposedly, and he spent millions of dollars restoring it.

There are many magnificent relics, such as the Sacred Cenote, an ancient observatory and the Temple of Kukulcan, a god whose symbol is a serpent wearing magnificent feathers. Kukulcan was the god of hope and emerging life and he was thought to fertilize the very breath of life. He was also the god of medicine and healing.

However, Chichen-Itza, more than any other site in the Yucatan, represents a juncture of Mayan civilization with the Toltec civilization. The Toltecs may have conquered the Mayans in battle and that is another theory as to why the culture disappeared from the face of the earth as it did. The Mayans fought whatever tribes were in the vicinity, and took many captives, but for the most part, it seems as if they stayed in or near the Yucatan during that span of almost two millenia.

One of the most famous sites at Chichen-Itza is the Temple of a Thousand Columns which consists of a thousand obelisks, each standing over ten feet tall, in a courtyard next to a pyramid. Each column is said to represent a warrior. Those obelisks were erected by the Toltecs, not the Mayans. The Toltecs weren't builders like the Mayans were, but they did erect many of the structures now found at Chichen-Itza.

Chichen-Itza was also home to one of the gigantic sacred Ball

Courts, which is 309 feet long and 114 feet wide. Two large hoops stood 23 feet in the center and the goal of the game was to get an object, shaped liked a ball, but said to have been a skull, into the hoop, not using hands to do so. Although no one knows too much about how the game was played, what is a well-known fact is that the losers were put to death.

One of the things for which the Mayans are most respected is their knowledge of astronomy and astrology. Their calendar and their mathematical computations are generally regarded as being incredibly accurate, even by today's standards. Some people think the world is going to come to an end in December of 2012 because that is when the Mayan calendar ends.

One of the natural phenomenons which the Mayans created through the use of their knowledge of astronomy and how the sun and the earth travel in predictable paths through the universe is the snake which seems to slither down the Temple of Kukulcan on March 21 and September 21 of each year for exactly 34 minutes. The light from the sun shines at exactly the right angle to give the impression of a snake coming out of the top of the temple and traveling down the pyramid, to its base, and disappearing into the ground. The snake was a symbol of fertility and signaled that it was time to plant, or harvest.

We stayed in Chichen-Itza for several days and swam in the cenote. Matthew was surprised they let us do that because it was such a sacred place. We were allowed to swim in any and all of the cenotes we came across, and we swam at most, if not all of the cenotes we found.

After going to Chichen-Itza, we went to Merida, which was the main stronghold of the Spanish in the Yucatan in the early days. Since it is inland by some 40 or 50 miles it was not susceptible to attack by pirates, as was Campeche, Tulum and other coastal towns, so it doesn't have walls around it. It was established in 1542, two years after Campeche. Construction of the oldest cathedral in Mexico and the second oldest in all of North America, St. Ildefonso, which still stands, was begun in 1561.

The Spanish made Merida their headquarters for ruling the Yucatan for centuries and built many of the magnificent structures that still stand in the central plaza today. Whatever Mayan structures were there had been dismantled and the stones were used to create the

Spaniards' buildings. We weren't too interested in seeing the large houses and the architecture, so we didn't stay long. Instead, we went to see Dzibilchaltun, a Mayan city located not far from Merida on the way to Progreso.

Jorge at the Temple of the Seven Dolls at Dzibilchaltun.

We saw more iguana there than at any other ruin. After spending the day in the city of Merida, which is now inhabited by over a million people, it was quite a contrast to be standing at the top of the Mayan temple of the Seven Dolls at Dzhihcholtun and watch the sun set, just the three of us, from where we had been earlier that day. Merida is less than an hour from Progreso and after the sun had gone down we were on our way to visit with my family in Progreso, which was one of the last legs on our journey.

Manny's older brother, Otto, who is my oldest cousin, was there, as well as Gabriel. He had become a helicopter pilot and had made enough money to allow him to buy a place in Progreso, not far from the malecon, where people could dance, drink beer and socialize. It was called "La Carioca."

None of us had seen Otto for a while and we wanted to spend some time with him. We got together with a bunch of our friends, too, and had a good time at La Carioca with him. Tourists hadn't found it yet so no one other than locals were there.

Matthew had made it through the worst part of the Yucatan,

camping in the jungles and eating meals that often consisted of only fresh fish, edible plants and the juices from green coconuts, without any problem with Montezuma's revenge, but drinking and eating salsa and fresh vegetables in Progreso got to him and he got as sick as could be. None of us knew any doctors and Matthew didn't have enough money to pay for one even if we could get him in to see one, but we did know a guy who worked in a pharmacy. So after a couple of days, without any signs of improvement, we told Matthew that we had called a doctor and he was going to come see him after his office was closed later that night.

About ten o'clock that night, our friend came over and he gave Matthew a shot of something, and we still don't know what it was, in his butt. The next day, Matthew started getting better. He thought it was a real doctor and was pleased with what we had done for him.

Two days later, we were at a friend's house drinking beer and we ordered some pizza. The guy who gave Matthew the shot also worked at the pizza place part-time and he delivered the pizza to us. Matthew saw him and said, "The doctor delivers pizza, too?" and we all told him that was true. He didn't believe us, of course, but if we had told him that a pizza delivery guy was going to give him a shot to make him better, he might not have let him stick that needle in his backsides. We laughed and laughed about the pizza delivery guy who was a doctor on the side.

In Progreso, as in Campeche, Chetumal and other places we had been, men walked around with a sack of coconuts on their back. They sold the green coconuts and were called "coconut men." That was how they made money and lots of people bought them. We did every time we saw one. They sold the juice in some restaurants and bars, too. It was called coco frio. It was supposedly a cure for a hangover.

Men walked around selling milk, too. There were no large stores like Publix, Food Lion, Winn-Dixie or any of the others, as there are in the U.S., in rural Mexico, and it was not uncommon to see food and other items sold on the street by people walking the streets. The guy who sold the milk was called 'lecheran,' or the milk man. There were dozens of young women walking the streets with clothes, jewelry and other items for the tourists as well.

We left Progreso a few days before it was time for Matthew to fly back to the States. We decided to take a short-cut to get to Cancun. Matthew wanted to see the area around the Rio del Gartos, the River of Alligators, just because he liked the name. It is a very remote area, and very sparsely inhabited.

Rio Lagartos is on the way from Progreso to Cancun as crows fly, but there aren't any good roads leading to it. There are no cities nearby, other than Progreso to the west and Cancun to the east. That little car Matthew had rented had been beaten up but it kept on running. Of all the bad roads we were on during our trip through the Yucatan the worst was the one we encountered on the way to Rio Lagartos. Once we left the main highway running from Merida to Cancun there was no turning back. We thought things would improve but the road kept getting worse and worse. It went from being a paved road, to a hard-packed dirt road, to a grass road and to a road with soft sand. We kept going, thinking eventually we would come to a better road, but it never happened.

Finally, we sunk the car up to its axles in sand. We tried our best to dig ourselves out, with no success. We had no idea what we were going to do. We sat there for a while, trying to decide what to do, when a twelve year old boy came walking along. We didn't have to tell him what was wrong. He said he'd be right back. Half an hour later, he came back with a donkey, a stout rope and a guitar. The donkey pulled us out of the sand and we followed the boy and the donkey to a little town which was little more than a few huts with palm frond roofs, on the water. One of the huts sold food and drinks and we sat, ate and listened to him play guitar for the rest of the afternoon. When the boy left, we went swimming.

The Gulf of Mexico and the Caribbean Sea meet up around there. The mouth of the Rio del Gartos is fed by the two bodies of water and there are some powerful currents swirling around. We went swimming and soon felt that we were in way over our heads. We swam back in, staying closer to shore and not going any deeper than where we could touch bottom. No sooner had we come back to shallower water than we saw the largest dorsal fin and tail I had ever seen in my life. I have no idea what kind of shark it was, but it was right where we had been swimming only minutes before. It might have been a Bull shark, or a

Tiger shark, maybe even a Great White for all I know. It was huge. We got out of the water altogether at that point.

Later that afternoon, as it got closer to sundown, while we were on our way to Cancun on this single lane road, we came upon the ruins of an abandoned church. The roof had long since been torn off or destroyed in some way. We stopped when we saw a fire burning inside. We wanted to know how much further we had to go. If it was too far, we were going to spend the night there.

A couple of old men were huddled around a fire, cooking their dinner. That was undoubtedly their home for the night. We asked them how far it was to Cancun. They answered us in some kind of language we were barely able to understand. It wasn't a dialect of Spanish that either Manny or I had ever heard before. They told us in leagues how far it was. Who knows where they came from or what their lives had been like, but they were definitely from a different century.

We made it to Cancun in time for Matthew to board his plane without any problems. Manny was going to stay with me and our family in Progreso a while longer. After Matthew left, I told him I would see him again for more adventures in America. When he left, I decided to make plans to get myself back to Miami. That was in late May of 1993. A few days after the journey was over, I wrote another poem:

The Path

I open trails, breaking branches as I go;
My heart beats fast as I do;
I run from myself, I run to myself,
I run in search of myself;
I caress the stones and the flowers along the way;
I ask them if I am behaving properly;
I lie between darkness and shade;
I pursue my dreams as if that is my reality;
I embrace the danger in my wild adventures;
At night, I filter my dreams and my feelings
And I undress them with softness;
This life is a daily battle I sometimes win and I sometimes lose;

I strive to find what is a constant in my life,
always wanting for something more;
Every loss, every failed experience, takes a
piece of my heart and my soul;
I shake hands with the victor without complaint
or sorrow;
I awaken each day, ready to learn from what
has been and find what is to be;
What am I looking for? Where am I going?
I seek to find what is real and not imaginary,
but is not reality an elusive goal?;
It does me no good to dream great thoughts
and then lose them somewhere in the depths of my subconscious mind;
In the end, what I seek is to find the best in me and look for the best
in those I meet, and enjoy this life I have been given in the process.

Chapter Six

Newport

After Matthew left, Manny stayed with me at my parent's house for a couple of weeks and then he, too, left to go back to the U.S. I felt a strong desire to return to America with them. I wanted to be in the United States. I felt as if I belonged there. I had learned how to speak English fairly well and I had learned how to survive in the U.S. I felt confident that I could safely travel in the United States and I felt that the United States was my adopted home, especially at Aunt Elba's or with my brother, Romeo. I was always at home at either place.

I decided to go to Michigan to be with my brother. Every time I left, as I was making preparations to leave, my parents would say to me, "Jorge, some day you will have to settle down." They were very concerned about my safety and worried if they would ever see me again. Both of my parents cried every time I left. My father would always ask me, "Jorge, why do you have to go?" and I would always respond, "Padre, mi tengo que ir," or "I must go." I always left with little more than a pack on my back, carrying everything I owned or would need.

A few weeks later, I flew back to Toronto. My brother drove across the bridge separating Detroit from Toronto, picked me up at the airport, and we drove back together. At the time, no visa was required to enter Canada for Mexican citizens, so I was allowed to enter into Canada on my Passport and from there, with my valid Michigan driver's license, I had no trouble crossing over into the United States.

In fact, that summer, while I was living with my brother and his family, I took a job at a mall in Toronto and worked as a security guard. I drove back and forth across the border every day, all summer long. Looking back on things, it's kind of ironic that I was not only able to get in and out of the U.S. into Canada so easily but I worked as a security guard to boot.

When the cold weather came, I took a bus to Miami and Aunt Elba's. I avoided planes and trains but I felt safe on a Greyhound Bus. The weather in Miami was no hotter than it was in Progreso, but I preferred to work at night, with few exceptions. I never had any trouble finding a job in Miami. That winter was no different. In early April of the next year, when spring had sprung, I headed back north.

It was now the spring of 1994. Not long after getting to Michigan I received word from Manny that our friend Matthew Sky had been in a bad accident in California. He had fallen off a horse and was now paralyzed from the waist down. I knew that doing dangerous things could have bad consequences, and Matthew loved to live dangerously, but it disturbed me very deeply that he was hurt so badly. I planned to see him as soon as I could, but he was in a hospital in the state of Washington. His parents lived somewhere in Florida and I would have to wait for him to come home to see him.

Later that year, after I was back in Miami, Manny found out from Matthew's sister, Rebecca, who lived in Miami and worked on South Beach, that Matthew had been transferred from the hospital in Washington to Jackson Memorial Hospital in Miami. As soon as I found out I went to see him. On the day I went to see him his whole family, or most of it, was there to see him as well.

He came from a big family, but I had only met Rebecca before that time. He had two brothers and six sisters and all but the oldest brother and two of his sisters were there, as I recall. I returned many times while he was hospitalized and became friends with the whole family, most of whom lived in Rhode Island and Massachusetts. He was quite depressed about his situation and didn't want to see anybody, but he was glad to see me.

Matthew explained to me that on the day he got hurt he had ridden his horse to check on some people who were camping in Yosemite. Some other guides were working that trip but he was a supervisor and he wanted to make sure everything was alright. It had rained earlier in the day and the ground was wet. His horse hit the root of a tree and slipped sideways causing Matthew to fall off. Matthew landed on his back, on top of the root, and the horse landed on top of him, damaging the spinal cord in the vicinity of T-11. He lost the use of his legs as a result of the accident.

He told me how he was in the woods overnight before anyone was able to find him. He was air-lifted out by helicopter the next day and then flown to the closest hospital that treated spinal cord injuries and had an available bed, which was in Seattle. He had been in hospitals for well over a year, waiting for his injury to stabilize. The procedure to put rods in his back, which would allow him to sit in a wheel chair and use his arms, failed two times. The doctors had to wait six months after each attempt to see if it was successful or not. When I saw him, he was in a specially designed bed, in a prone position, hoping that the procedure would be successful on the third try.

After seeing him, and meeting his family, I wrote another poem.

Pulse and Reflex

You and I have shared many good times together.
We both love the beauty of nature, and we
appreciate well its darkness and dangers.
Don't despair over what has been lost, and don't
lose hope for what the future holds;
Today, together with the sun and the stars, I pray for you;
I admire you and other people who move fast,
sometimes too fast and don't see fear as they go;
I want to transform you with my good thoughts;
I treasure companions, like you, who have
traveled with me on adventures;
Companions who have offered me support for my journey;
You seek the truth, as I do;
I want to travel with you again, as we did before;
Teach me how to walk by your side as we once did;
And together we will go farther and see further than we did before;
And I will help you and others who, like me, have at times lost their way;
And I seek wisdom and guidance in my efforts to stay on the
path of life, full of thrills and adventure, with knowledge and
appreciation that it can all end quite suddenly at any time.

I spent the winters of '95 and '96 in Miami and the summers in Michigan. In the fall of 1997, after the landscaping job in Michigan ended as the cold weather was arriving, I received a call from Matthew's younger brother David, asking me to give him a ride to Miami. I agreed. He was going to school at Holy Cross Junior College in South Bend, Indiana, which wasn't far from where I was, but when I picked him up he asked me to take him to Newport, Rhode Island before going back to Miami.

Although Rhode Island was far out of the way, since I had never been there before, I agreed. I wasn't in a hurry and it would give me an opportunity to see another part of the United States. It took a full day to get there but, while there, I was able to meet the rest of Matthew's family, who were his oldest brother, John; his oldest sister, Mary; and another sister, Joy. We spent a couple of weeks there and I enjoyed myself in Newport. I felt very much at home since Newport was a sailing community and I was a sailor. David and the others told me I would have no trouble getting a job in Newport during the summer months if I was interested.

I spent the winter in Miami, again, working in a restaurant and playing soccer as often as I could. I stayed with Manny and his mother, my Aunt Elba, again. She was always happy to have me. I was like a son to her and during those years she saw me more than she did Otto or Gabriel.

The next summer, which was the summer of 1998, I went to Newport instead of Michigan. My brother was having some problems at home and, though he told me I was welcome, I got the feeling that it might be better if I didn't go there.

Both Matthew and David had talked to Joy's husband and they told me that I could to go to work for their brother-in-law who built and repaired houses in Newport. I could sleep in one of the houses they were repairing if I wanted to. He usually worked alone and wouldn't have to put me on a payroll, take out for social security, pay workers compensation and the rest. He would just pay me cash at the end of every week. I was able to start whenever I got there and quit whenever I wanted to. I arrived at the beginning of June.

Newport is a small city with a population of less than 30,000 people and it is actually an island connected to the mainland by bridges. I didn't know any of the history of the city but it is the home of the Naval War College and the United States' Navy's Training Center, among other things. I visited those places just to see the boats and learn more about it.

In part because of its location, Newport had a long history of sailing, much like Boston or New York, but not all of it was good. Dating back to the 1600s and early 1700s pirates used it as a base of operations. Many outlaws were hung there and buried on nearby Goat Island.

Newport was supposedly the center of the slave trade for all of New England and was part of the "triangle trade" by which sugar and molasses from the Caribbean were brought to Rhode Island and made into rum, which was then transported to West Africa and exchanged for slaves. There is a cemetery in the heart of the city where many slaves who had died en route were buried. I visited there too. To its credit, the state of Rhode Island banned slave trading as early as 1787, not long after the Revolutionary War ended. Supposedly over 700 different ship-owners operated a slave trade out of Newport at its peak.

By the early 1900s, many of the wealthiest people in the country owned mansions in Rhode Island and spent summers there, including the Vanderbilts and the Astors. In the 1850s, during the potato famine, a large number of Irish settled there, undoubtedly as household servants for the rich or workers for the factories and farms in the area.

The southern part of the city became a predominantly Irish neighborhood and it still is. Matthew's mother was Irish and that was where she was born. John F. Kennedy and Jacqueline Bouvier were married there. That's where Joy and her husband lived and that's where I lived that first summer. There were several Irish bars within walking distance. I think I was the only Mexican but I felt welcome. Joy's husband and I drank a bottle of tequila together the day I met him.

Newport calls itself the sailing capital of the world, which may be an exaggeration, but it has more of the 12 meter boats that won the America's Cup in its harbors than anywhere else in the world. Of course, American boats won the Cup for about a hundred and fifty years in a row and since many of the Cup races were held in the waters off of Newport it makes sense that most of the boats would be berthed there. I liked to go down and just look at those magnificent boats and, on weekends, I'd watch the races as best I could from shore using binoculars. There were many, many other sailing boats there, too. I didn't get to sail much there but I watched a lot of races.

I liked Newport. I was staying with people who knew me through Matthew and David and, because no one knew that I was an illegal alien, I felt safe. No one bothered me and I didn't bother anyone. I met a lot of people through the Sky family and at the bars. I spent a lot of time with a nice woman there that summer but that fizzled when the season ended and I went back to Miami.

I don't know why I was unable to develop a more permanent and lasting relationship with a woman during the years after my relationships with Mary and Rayna ended. I figured it was because I traveled too much. Everywhere I went I was around beautiful women. Most came from very wealthy families. I was, at best, a Mexican who worked at repairing houses, painting houses, cleaning yards or other such tasks. In the words of the song sung by country western singer Mickey Gilley in the movie Urban Cowboy, maybe I was looking for love in all the wrong places.

Because I was illegal, I was always careful not to get into any trouble, and if there were ever any police officers or law enforcement officers of any kind, I would always leave. I didn't see my parents for long periods of time, and I missed them and, even though I was around friends in Newport, it was a lonely time for me. When I was feeling particularly low, I wrote poetry. I never let anyone else read any of it. It was written just for me.

Chapter Seven

SHIPWRECKED

That fall, when I returned to Miami, which was the fall of 1998, my brother Romeo was there at my Aunt Elba's house. He had just gone through a divorce and was about to leave to go back to Mexico. He wanted me to join him and, though I didn't want to leave, I couldn't tell him no. He had been too good to me for too many years for me to do that, so I went.

We drove back to Progreso in a Ford Mustang I had bought. While home, I spent time working with my father, writing and doing photography work. I took a few people on trips to photograph the Mayan temples and other places of interest, like I did before, but mostly I stayed at home. I had been away for several years and my parents weren't getting any younger, though they both were still quite active and healthy. I enjoyed the time being with them.

My older sister was now a teacher in a local school and doing quite well. My younger sister was now a teenager. It was good to have Romeo at home, too. It was a nice time for my parents as well as they had all of their children at home at the same time.

One day, a month after I arrived, an American who was looking for a man who spoke fluent English and knew about boats, like I did, came to the house asking for me. One of my friends had directed him to me. He offered me a large sum of money to assist him in refurbishing a boat. It was a fifty eight foot long 1957 Peacemaker, a classic wooden boat, with two inboard 500 horsepower Detroit diesel engines.

I had learned a few things over the years about fixing up boats and I was able to do what he wanted to have me do. There were others who had better technical skills but my contribution was primarily going to be directing the workers who did not speak English and making sure the job was done right. I was like the agent of the owner, or a liason of sorts between him and the workers.

The boat was located in a shipyard in Progreso and it was a perfect job for me. The pay was good. I could walk to work, and I enjoyed doing that kind of work.

I spent the next four months working with the others fixing up that boat. When it was finished, my boss was happy with my work and wanted me to go with him on the trip across the Gulf of Mexico to Florida. The problem was that I didn't think that it was seaworthy, even after we fixed it, and I told him so.

I told him that it was a good boat for rivers, lakes and bays, but not in heavy seas. He assured me that it would make the journey with no problem. Although I was initially hired only to help fix it up, he coaxed me into going on the trip by offering me more money to do so. Despite my fears that the boat wasn't seaworthy, I agreed to go. I was ready to return to the United States and I needed the money, so he didn't have to twist my arm too much.

Peacemaker before repairs

Jorge with Peacemaker after repairs were completed

We left in early June, the owner, myself and three other men. We had no problems on the cruise from Progreso to the Isla de Mujeres and I thought to myself that if the weather was good and the sea was calm we could make it to Miami. We checked the weather and saw signs of a storm in the Gulf, so we waited several days for the weather to clear before attempting to cross the Gulf.

After the bad weather left, and after checking the weather and seeing no signs of a problem, we left at midnight under clear skies. Top speed for the boat was 10 or 11 knots. We expected to complete the journey in a day and a half. It's not even 200 miles from Isla de Mujeres to Key West and we were taking a direct path to Key West, not like we had to do in a sail boat and tack back and forth as the winds dictated. We expected to pass about forty miles from Cabo San Antonio, which is the furthest point to the west on the island of Cuba on the way, which was the half-way point.

As soon as we got close to Cuba, the waters of the Gulf became extremely rough due to a particularly bad afternoon thunderstorm. The seas rose to twenty foot swells and the boat slowed to 2 to 3 knots. I knew we were in trouble and hoped the weather would pass before something bad happened. Unfortunately, we weren't that lucky.

Just prior sunrise, while it was still pitch dark, the mechanic came to me since I was at the wheel and said "Nos hestamos hundiendo," which meant that we were sinking. The heavy seas had torn a hole in the lower bow, which was made of wood, which I couldn't see.

I immediately went with the mechanic to the engine room and saw that salt water was covering over half of the two engines and water was coming in fast. My first reaction was that we were going to die. We had lost our electronic capabilities, including the antenna, due to the storm and high winds. We were too far out at sea to be able to summon help. All we had left was a ship-to-shore radio and that didn't carry too far.

The mechanic said we had to fix the leak by ourselves. We had to stop the water from coming in and we had to get the water that was already in the boat out. The bilge pumps weren't working and we couldn't bail the water out by hand. The lights were still on but only very dimly so it was hard to see what we were doing. The owner said there was a big water pump with a compressor on board but it hadn't been used in years.

I located it and saw that it was very rusty. The mechanic said that if we wanted to live that was our only hope. He said the boat would sink very quickly if we didn't get the water out of the pump room fast. All we had was a rubber raft and life jackets.

While the others did what they could to fix the leak and stop the water from continuing to come in, I changed the spark plugs, cleaned the wires and did what I could to get the old pump to work so that we could get the water out.

When I had done all that I could, the mechanic and I took turns pulling on the rope to start the compressor. After several minutes it started. We threw a hose through the hatch and started pumping water. It saved the boat and our lives. After an hour or so the engine room was cleared of most of the water but water was still coming in. The patch job was just that, a patch. It would take some time to repair the damage done to the hull and we didn't have the materials to do the job right.

Fortunately for us, the engines never stopped. It was raining and we were all soaking wet, and shivering. Our spirits brightened a bit when the skies began to lighten in the east, but it was still raining. The five of us discussed our situation and it was agreed that we had been fortunate but we would never make it all the way to Key West. We decided to head for Cuba, which was thirty some miles away.

However, we knew that Cabo San Antonio was nothing more than a small fishing village and that we would have to make it to Havana to find what we needed to have the boat repaired. Our plan was to get the coast line of Cuba in sight and to stay as close to the coast as we could. It was still a dangerous situation we were in because the weather was still very bad and there are many reefs along the coast of Cuba.

Once we got close enough to shore we were able to make contact with Cuban authorities through our ship to shore radio we reported our condition. They asked if we could make it to Havana. We told them that we thought we could and that we didn't need a rescue. It was going to take us two full days to make it to Havana at the rate we were going, which was very slow. By sunrise of the following day, we were sixteen miles north of Pinar del Rio, but we were still about a hundred miles from Havana.

The waves had diminished some and we started to go faster, but another thunderstorm hit us again that afternoon. As I was standing in the kitchen, making coffee for the group, the boat hit a reef, knocking me to the ground. The boat came to a sudden stop. When it hit the reef the boat had veered towards the land and into shallow water. I got up and ran on deck. I saw pieces of wood floating by and knew we were done.

The owner yelled to me telling me that I should put on my mask, get in the water and fix the problem. I told him that I needed to get my passport first. The only reason the boat hadn't sunk was because we were in shallow water. He put it in reverse but the boat didn't move. He knew I was right and called the people at the marina in Pinar del Rio to report our situation.

Once the sun came up some fisherman came by and offered to help but there was nothing they could do. About five hours later, a Cuban naval vessel arrived and the captain told us we had two options, either remain on the boat and operate it to safety or the Navy would take control of the boat. Our boat was in no condition to keep going, which meant we had only one option.

We boarded their ship and they took us to a naval station at Pinar del Rio. I could hear them as they made calls and began to organize a rescue of the vessel. The owner thought that he would probably never see his boat again.

Once we were safely on shore we were turned over to Cuban Army authorities. We were kept for a day on the military base there while they towed the vessel in to the port and inspected it. They talked to the owner about the situation but they weren't going to fix it, the owner would have to make arrangements to have the boat fixed or destroyed. The Cuban Navy had done its job and was no longer involved with the problem. There would be fines to pay and if the fines weren't paid the boat would be kept to cover the costs involved with the rescue operation.

The next day an Army Lieutenant informed us that we would be taken to Havana for questioning. We had no idea what we were going to be questioned about. Maybe they thought we were spies or something. We didn't know. We were taken on a military bus to Havana and turned over to their Customs and Immigration personnel. At that time we were told that we would be held in custody until their investigation was completed.

The owner became upset and said there was no reason for us to be held according to international law. He told them that we should be allowed to leave immediately. We hadn't done anything wrong, we had been the victims of bad weather, that's all. The officer in charge said that we were in Cuba and we would be dealt with according to Cuban law.

We were then placed in a jail where, presumably, they held criminals. They put us in a cell by ourselves and told us it was an International Detention Center. From what we could gather, there were many other people there who were in the same situation, though it was difficult to talk to them through the walls. I was very upset and worried about what might happen to us.

The first night we were there a riot broke out when some of the prisoners tried to force their release by capturing one of the jailers. The regular Army was called in to deal with the situation. We couldn't see anything, but we heard the screams. Once the Army arrived, the situation was brought under control.

We thought we would only be there for a day or two but after five days we were asking questions and not getting any answers. The jail was underground and we had no windows to the outside world. It was surprisingly cool under ground where we were, but not being able to see the sun was a problem for us.

One hour per day we were taken to a room that had a skylight and we were allowed to smoke a cigarette and see the sun. The food consisted of rotten rice, rotten beans, stale bread, no meat, and water to drink. I refused to eat at first, but after several days hunger set in and I ate the bread and drank the water. We were given dirty mattresses to put on metal cots with springs in them. The sheets and blankets looked as if they hadn't been cleaned in a long while.

One morning, a jailer came to my bed and told me that I had to make it. I was still sleeping and I told him I would make my bed as soon as I was awake. He grabbed me by my arm and forcibly pulled me out of bed and walked me down the hall and put in the general population with guys from Angola, Pakistan, South America and other places. I stayed for several hours until the owner gave the jailer a couple of packs of cigarettes and the man let me back in the cell with my mates.

After two weeks we were allowed to contact our embassies. The owner contacted a U.S. representative at Guantanimo and he got out right away. I was allowed to contact the Mexican embassy in Havana. The other guys and I were to be immediately released to return to Mexico but when I told them that I wanted to go the United States I was kept for another two days, by myself, in a cell. When I was released I was taken to the airport to travel by plane to Miami with the owner. He had made all the arrangements.

We flew on a commercial airline from Cuba to Grand Cayman where we changed planes and then from Grand Cayman it was on to Miami. I told myself that if I got in America I was going to stay in and never leave.

Chapter Eight

Back in the U.S.A.

As I was flying from Cuba to Miami I was thinking that since I had been allowed into the country even after U.S. Customs and everybody else checked me out so thoroughly that I must be legal, or at least not on the radar screen, and that I might not have any trouble getting through Customs. If not, I'd be on my way back to Mexico. When I arrived at the airport in Miami I was pulled out of line by a Cuban-American Immigration officer.

He asked me what nationality I was. I told him I was an American. He said, "You're not an American! You're a fucking Mexican!" I told him Mexico is north of the Equator and that I was a North American. He scoffed at me and saw no humor in what I had said.

He questioned me for over an hour about what I was planning to do in Miami. I told him I was going to stay with my Aunt and my cousins, just visiting. He asked if I planned to work while there and I answered, "Of course not." When he was finished questioning me, he said that he didn't believe a word I said but he stamped my Passport and visa and let me enter the country. My ten year visa was to expire shortly after that and that was my last entry into the United States that was arguably legal.

Since I got into Miami late in the day, after calling my Aunt and finding out that Manny was working in a restaurant in South Beach, I hitched a ride straight to South Beach. I planned to get a ride home with him. I had no money whatsoever on me and no clothes except those on my back. I had lost everything I had between the shipwreck and the Cuban jail.

When I arrived in South Beach, I saw Rebecca Sky, who was a licensed massage therapist, working a booth she had set up on a vacant lot. There was a long line of people waiting to see her. She asked if I could help and I agreed. I worked the rest of the afternoon and most of that night doing massages for people. That training I received back in Mexico while I was playing soccer paid off. I went home with over $150 that night.

I found a job washing boats at the Miami Beach Marina. Some of the boats I washed were right next to the slips where U.S. Customs boats were berthed and I talked on a daily basis with the Customs Officers. I didn't want to talk to them but I figured that it would be better if I talked to them than if I avoided them or averted their glances. I'm basically a friendly person and I don't have any trouble talking to people. I'm sure that comes from me being a guide for so long and always meeting new people. It worked as they never questioned me or caused me any difficulties whatsoever.

At the marina, there were boats for rent as well as commercial boats for hire, like for fishing trips, and then private boats, too. There were some very expensive boats at the marina, and those were the ones I washed. I met people like Kevin Costner, O.J. Simpson and many others. I was even interviewed by a local television station while I was washing a boat as a hurricane was approaching.

When I saw O.J. Simpson I spoke to him. The people I was working with told me I shouldn't have done that. They said I was befriending a murderer. I think I was the only person who spoke to him. Most people looked away and didn't say a word to him.

I never had a problem getting a job in Miami. I gave them a fake social security number at times and at other times they never asked. Now there were plenty of times when I went for a job and was told that since I didn't have a green card or papers showing that I was legally in the country they wouldn't hire me, but once I was given a chance by someone and they saw how I worked, they wanted to keep me as an employee. Sometimes I had two jobs at a time. It was always easy to get a job at a restaurant.

That winter I worked at a very popular restaurant called Nimo's at night and at the marina during the day. I worked as a busboy and bar-back. A well-known chef from Philadelphia worked there and he became a very good friend of mine. I always wanted to be a bartender. It was better than washing dishes, waiting tables or being a busboy. Being a bar-back was like being a bartender in training. That was my first opportunity to do that. Everybody knew me and no one suspected that I was an illegal alien.

I went back to Newport again that summer, working with Joy's husband, doing the same things as the year before, and returned to Miami in the fall to work at the Marina again. I worked at a different restaurant that winter and I was able to get my job at the Marina back. It was good work and I loved being around the water.

In March of the following year, which would have been 2001, a friend of mine named Guillermo, who was from Mexico City, asked me to help him sail a trimaran to Cancun. He had bought it in Ft. Lauderdale and needed my help fixing it up. I refused to make the journey with him at first, because I wasn't ready to leave Miami, but I agreed to help him get the boat ready to go.

We worked on the boat for several weeks getting it ready and all the time he kept insisting that I join him. Although I had two jobs and was happy in Miami, eventually he talked me into it. I loved sailing and I agreed to go with him.

I wasn't afraid that I wouldn't be able to get back into the country because I could make it in so easily by flying to Toronto and coming in that way. My Michigan driver's license was still valid. They're good for six or eight years, I forget which, and I had renewed it once.

A trimaran sails much faster than a single hull sailboat. Though there wasn't much of a cabin or a place to sleep as nice as on some of the other boats I had been on, it was fun sailing it. We made the trip without any trouble at all in about three days. Again, a strong tailwind helped us.

At that point in my life, I felt as if the United States was my home. I was welcome in Miami with my Aunt Elba and in Newport, and in Michigan too, even though Romeo wasn't there as much anymore. I was still friendly with his ex-wife and I was still the uncle of his children. I wasn't straying too far out of my small circle of family and friends. I was happy with my life. I missed my family and Mexico at times, but I preferred being in the United States.

It wasn't about the money, as I wasn't making all that much more than I could have been making in Mexico. It was more about the life style, the excitement, the adventure of daily living, and always about a feeling of traveling, moving with the earth, following a path I felt was right for me, even though it didn't seem as if I had a destination or even a purpose. My parents didn't know what I was doing or why I was doing it.

To me, living is a spiritual journey, just being who I felt that I was, doing what I felt I should be doing, and being as nice to people I met along the way. I always appreciated all the nice things people did for me, and I befriended many nice people along the way. I felt that I was an ambassador for my country and my people and I always welcomed an opportunity to tell Americans about Mexico, the Mayan civilization and about my heritage.

Also, although I knew I was in the country illegally, I felt as if I really didn't need a green card. I could come and go as I pleased. I felt as if something would happen and I would, somehow, some way, eventually become a citizen. I didn't know how that would happen, I just knew that if I stayed out of trouble and didn't commit any crimes, that things were going to work out for me. I was sure of it.

Chapter Nine

From Sea to Shining Sea

In 2001, before the September 11 tragedy and before security got much tighter for people entering the United States, I decided to do some traveling and see more of the United States, so I flew into Toronto, crossed over into the United States, and bought a ticket out of Detroit on a Greyhound bus for Seattle, Washington, even though I had never been there and didn't know anyone who lived out there.

I could have gone back to Newport, and I could have stayed in Michigan, but Matthew Sky had told me how beautiful the western part of the United States was and I just wanted to see it for myself. I had been to Colorado, and that was spectacular, but that was as far west as I had been. Besides, without Romeo there in Michigan, it wouldn't have been the same, and Joy Sky and her husband were having some marital problems and I was told that it might be best if I didn't work there with him again that summer. I probably could have found another job in Newport because I had met so many people the summers before, but it seemed like a good time to travel and I did.

The trip took two days. As soon as I arrived I went to the day-labor pool, looking for a job. As I was standing in line a man came up to me and asked if I would help him paint a barn. I agreed. We drove for an hour in his truck to a Valley outside of Seattle. He had an room above the barn where I could stay and I worked for him until the barn was finished, which took a couple of weeks to complete. After the barn was painted and some other smaller jobs he had me do were done, he found me a job at a nearby ranch working with horses and cows. I cleaned out stalls and did whatever work was needed on the ranch. Mostly I was a helper. It was a beautiful place to live. The ranch wasn't too far from Mt. Rainier and the views were magnificent.

On days when I wasn't working and the weather was good, I liked to go hiking into the mountains. On days when the weather was bad, I'd catch a bus into Seattle and see the sights. It was a beautiful city though there weren't too many Mexicans there. In fact, at most everyplace I'd been in the U.S up to that point, whenever anyone I was with used an ATM, it always asked about a language preference and the choice was either English or Spanish. In Seattle, it was English or Japanese, or maybe it was Chinese. I didn't know. There were a lot of Asians there.

One day, as I was sitting on a bench in a park in Seattle, drinking coffee I had just bought from a Starbucks, overlooking the waters of the Puget Sound, watching people come off ferry boats, I saw a group of over a dozen uniformed law enforcement officers of some kind get off a boat and come walking towards me. I didn't know it at the time, but their offices were two floors above the Starbucks store and they had to walk right past me to get to the building. Being paranoid about having police officers anywhere near me, I tried to think of a way I could leave without drawing attention to myself. It all happened so fast, there was nothing I could do except sit there and act as normally as I could.

I saw from their uniforms that they were all U.S. Customs and Immigration agents. Every one of them walked past within a few feet of me. They all said hello to me and I said hello right back to them. I had a tour book of the Seattle area in my hands and I kept my head down, pretending to be reading it. The last two were older than the others. They seemed to be the ones in charge.

One of the two older men stopped and started to talk to me in Spanish. He asked where I was from and I told him Michigan, since I was carrying a valid Michigan driver's license. He asked me what I was doing in Seattle. I told him I was just visiting and that I had never been there before. He wanted to know what I did in Michigan, how long I was staying in Seattle, where I was staying, what I was doing while there and all kinds of questions, like he knew that I was an illegal Mexican working without proper papers, which I was, of course, and he was just waiting for me to make a mistake, say the wrong thing, and give him an excuse to arrest me.

He was asking his questions in a nice, friendly way, but every time I answered a question he had another question for me. After answering the tenth question, I looked down at my cup, saw that it was nearly empty and said that I needed to get a re-fill. I stood, excused myself, and walked towards the Starbucks. He followed me, still talking to me all the while, into the store.

I asked the woman at the counter for a re-fill and for some other things, like a roll or pastry which needed to be cooked or heated up, anything that would take her a little time to get. I then asked if they had a restroom. She pointed to where it was and I told her I would be right back.

Once I was inside the restroom, I looked for another way to get out and noticed that there was a door at the back of the room that was an emergency exit. I didn't know if the alarm would go off if I used it, but I was getting out of there one way or another. When I pushed open the door, fortunately, no bells went off, or at least none that I heard. I took off running down an alley and past some railroad tracks as fast as I could.

I went back to the bus station and got on the first bus back out to the Valley and the ranch where I was working. When you are an illegal, you have to be very careful all of the time, and I was.

I always avoided police officers and never told anybody what my situation was. When I told Romeo about that incident he told me that the circle was growing smaller and that I should do the right thing and do whatever was necessary to become a citizen. I knew that it took five years to go through the process of applying for citizenship and I couldn't very well say that I had been living in the country, working illegally, so I never did it. When the summer ended, at the first sign of cold weather, I took the long bus ride from Seattle to Miami and spent the winter there.

The next summer, which was the summer of 2002, I went back to Rhode Island, but I went to work with David Sky on Block Island instead of staying in Newport. We took a ferry from Newport to get to it. It took about an hour to get there. The ferry from Newport only runs in the summer and few people live there during the winter.

Block Island is 13 miles out in the Atlantic. It was 13 miles from Rhode Island and also only 14 miles east of Long Island, New York. A little over a thousand people live there in the summer, but thousands of people visit the island every day during the summer. The island was named after a Dutch explorer named Adrian Block who charted it in 1614. It is listed by the Nature Conservancy as one of the "Last Great Places" in the Western Hemisphere.

The only town on the island is New Shoreham. It's a popular place to be in the summer and good for bicycling, hiking, sailing, fishing, and lying in the sun on any one of its many beaches. The only electricity to the island was provided by diesel generators and as we would find out they sometimes weren't adequate to meet the demand.

David is an artist and his specialty is large murals on walls or on the sides of buildings. One of his creations can be found at the University of Florida's Museum of Natural History. It is a mural depicting an underwater scene with fish, turtles and other sea life. He also sells paintings but he had to have a day job until his paintings could provide him with more income. Until then, he and I would be painting houses and buildings. We'd split whatever moneys we'd get. He never knew, at least not then, that I was an illegal. No one did. The money was much better on Block Island but things were more expensive also.

It was while I was working with David that I was able to start spending time at the sailing center on Block Island. After getting off work, since the sun didn't go down until 8:00 or so, I spent a couple of hours every day helping children learn how to sail and doing things around the marina. I helped with maintenance on the boats; I worked in the restaurants whenever they needed extra people to work a big party; I parked cars sometimes…I did whatever they asked me to do and I volunteered to do things before anyone asked me to do something. They were very happy with my work and told me I could have a job there the next summer, if I wanted.

There were many serious sailors with boats berthed in the harbor on Block Island and I met a number of them. Many of them would go up to Marblehead, Cohasset, Falmouth, Martha's Vineyard and Nantucket for races, like National events, but there were always races on weekends for all sizes and shapes of boats and people off Block Island, too. Although I was a sailor, I never had a chance to participate in any of the races that summer. I went sailing while there a few times, but that was it. The biggest event of the summer on the island was Block Island Race Week, a competitive, week-long sailboat race involving the biggest and best boats in America. That was fun to watch, though I would rather have been sailing in it.

There are two historic lighthouses on the island. One is on the northern tip and the other on the southern tip. It has been the site of many famous shipwrecks over the years, including a U.S. submarine and a German submarine during W.W. II, but the most famous shipwreck was in 1738. It became famous because John Whittier wrote a poem about it called "The Wreck of the Palatine." During World War II several artillery spotters were located on the island to keep a look-out for German submarines.

Whenever I had time off and wasn't at the sailing center, I liked to hike around the island. There were several bluffs that gave a great view of the ocean and whatever ships or boats were on the water. The best one, and the highest one, is Mohegan Bluffs which has 141 steps I had to climb to get to the top.

Many of the beaches were good for surfing, though many others were too rocky. The island has some impressive cliffs like Clayhead and Pots and Kettles. It's also a stopover place for birds migrating up and down the east coast. I was like one of the migrating birds, just stopping over for the summer. It was a nice place to be for me.

Though I was living in one of the most beautiful places on earth, doing something that I loved to do, I was not truly happy. Something was missing from my life. That something was a person to share it with. I knew that and I yearned to find it. I wrote a poem about how I felt.

Feelings

I am a poet who walks alone, as if in exile;
I am like a piece of cotton, dry and without flavor;
I find myself at this moment, in this place,
knowing that death will find me sometime and knowing
that before it does I want to navigate the
earth and ride the waves of the seas and have
an adventure like nobody before me;
Yet how many fears and failures, pain and sorrow

must I experience before I find someone to share those emotions with in a loving relationship?
How long must I live without loving? What is success if there is no joy?
And here I am, in this beautiful place, still seeking to find a mate for my soul.

I spent the winter in Miami again and the next summer I went back to Block Island, but this time I went to work at the Yacht Club, not with David. Again, I helped teach children to sail at their sailing center. I did maintenance on the boats, I worked in the restaurant, I painted buildings and I did whatever they asked me to do, but this time I got paid for it. They were very happy with me and told me I could have a job there whenever I wanted. I worked there for several summers.

Chapter Ten

CEDAR KEY, FLORIDA

In the spring of 2004, on my way up to Block Island for the summer, I drove across the state of Florida to the west coast to visit Matt Sky. He had finally recovered from his injury enough to be able to regain some of his independence and some of that sense of adventure I admired in him so much. He had bought a house just outside of Cedar Key, Florida and had been there for a few months. David was planning to meet me there and we were going to drive up to Block Island in separate cars after spending some time with Matt.

I hadn't owned a car in a few years and decided to buy one so that I wouldn't have to take public transportation as much. A friend of mine was leaving the country and had to sell his Volkswagen. I liked the Volkswagens. They weren't flashy, so they didn't attract any attention, and they were very reliable.

An old Volkswagen, even now, in Mexico is a prized possession. Anyone who has an old Volkswagen Beetle treats it like it was a Cadillac, Lexus or a Jaguar even. Of all the cars on the planet, I think Mexicans would like a Jaguar best. The jaguar is still considered to be god-like, but Volkswagens were priced right for my meager budget. His was a Jetta model. This was one of the original ones, too, made in 1979. After test-driving it, I bought it.

It was bigger than a compact, yet not as big as a sedan. 1979 was the first year they made them. It had a hatchback and was big enough that I could sleep in it if I had to. My Jetta was called a four-door sedan and had five-seats.

So I drove my Jetta across Alligator Alley to I-75 and then north through Tampa to U.S. 19 north through Homosassa Springs and Crystal River and then west on State Road 24 to Cedar Key. I left in the early evening, planning to drive through the night and get there sometime after midnight.

The road from U.S. 19 to Cedar Key is a two-lane highway, one lane in each direction, and it is very, very dark out there at night. The closest city is Gainesville, fifty miles to the east. Chiefland is twenty miles to the north and Crystal River is twenty miles to the south. The Gulf of Mexico is to the west, but there are miles and miles of empty stretches with nothing more than an occasional mobile home off to the side.

I drove my Jetta very slowly, taking good care of it, and I was driving slowly that night, stopping every now and then as deer ran across in front of me. I must have seen over fifty that night. Whenever I saw them standing by the side of the road, I slowed to a stop, never knowing if they were going to dart into the road or off into the scrub.

I had stopped to get gas in Crystal River. I had some dinner at a seafood restaurant and I was taking my time. I was in no hurry. I was going slow. It was well after midnight as I got to within ten miles of Matthew's home. I was paying attention, but I didn't know that there were feral pigs all over that part of the state and I didn't see any danger when I saw a black object off to the side of the road. I thought it was a box or a garbage bag.

The black object ran out in front of me and I hit it right smack in the middle of my Jetta's front grill. I was going almost fifty miles an hour at the time and barely had time to put my foot on the brake. My car came to a dead stop and my head hit the steering wheel.

I could have cried. I called Matthew and woke him up. He came to meet me. We surveyed the damage. It could have been worse for my Jetta but not for the pig. It was too heavy for us to load up and we left it off to the side of the road.

The next day I drove the vehicle in to the one mechanic in Cedar Key, who removed the grill. The radiator was pushed back into the belts and I had to get another radiator. Some belts had to be replaced too, but the motor wasn't damaged. It took several days to find a used radiator from a junk yard and to get things fixed, but it could have been much worse.

It had been eleven years since Matthew had been injured. Once the bones in his cervical spine melded together so that he could sit upright in a wheelchair he enrolled in school at the University of Florida to learn about computers. After he obtained his degree, he worked for a few years doing computer programming for a company in Orlando, but after he made enough money to buy a house, he gave that up. He just couldn't sit in front of a computer in a small cubicle in a big office. He belonged outside, in nature, and he found Cedar Key and had made that his home.

Cedar Key is two hours north of Tampa and I had been to Tampa once before, briefly. One of my Mexican friends had met a girl in Miami, and they had a brief romance which resulted in her becoming pregnant. He was a nice young man and he really wanted to do the right thing. So he asked Manny and me to take him to see her and meet her parents, who were migrant workers working somewhere not far from Tampa.

It was January and the workers were picking strawberries in the fields of Plant City, just outside of Tampa. One Sunday, we got up early and Manny and I drove him over so that he could see the girl and meet her family. When we got there, Manny and I stayed in the car as the young man, whose name was Wilfredo, knocked on the door to the trailer where she lived. Her father and her four brothers came out and they did not look happy to see him. In fact, they had guns in their hands.

I was driving Manny's car, a Ford Mustang, and I immediately did a U-turn in the dirt road, spinning tires and kicking up dust as I did. Wilfredo started running, yelling "Wait for me!" I slowed down about a quarter of the mile outside of the trailer park to let him in. We didn't stop until we were back in Miami Beach.

Other than that one time, I had never been to the west coast of Florida. Cedar Key is a small fishing village with a population of less than a thousand people, not close to anyplace and not on the way to anyplace, either. The one road into the town, State Road 24, ends at the Gulf of Mexico. Cedar Key is at the end of the road. It is 24 miles off of U.S. 19 so no one passes through Cedar Key on their way to any place else.

Matthew had bought himself a little house two miles outside of town. The living area was on the second floor. It had an elevator in the front for him to get up or down or he could use a long series of ramps he and David had built so he could roll himself in.

He had learned how to hoist himself into and out of a pick-up truck and had regained his independence. He also was able to fish out of a sit-on-top kayak. The three of us went out into the waters off of Shell Mound the next day. Shell Mound is a site built by indigenous people with clam shells and oyster shells. It is otherwise a completely flat terrain with marshes. There is a state preserve nearby called the Scrub, and that describes the area pretty well.

I caught a fish that was about as big as I was. It was a Black Drum and, although it wasn't considered good eating, there was no way I was throwing that fish back. We also caught several Redfish, a few Trout and some Whiting.

Jorge with Black Drum caught in the Gulf of Mexico off Cedar Key, Florida

Jorge fishing from a kayak off Cedar Key, Florida

Jorge with Matthew and Rebecca Sky in Cedar Key.

Jorge with David Sky

We broke bread that night, drank some cerveza and talked about the good times. After dinner, we went into town to a few of the local bars to listen to some music. Matthew had lost the use of his legs, but everything else worked and his spirits were back. He talked of returning to the mountains out west.

Matthew and David were big men. Both were over 6'4" tall, in fact. I am short, maybe five and a half feet tall, if that. The average Mayan male was supposedly no more than 5' tall. What height I have I got from my Spanish ancestors. They called me "Enanu de Uxmal," which meant the Dwarf of Uxmal. They thought it was funny. It never bothered me when they called me that. I considered it a compliment.

The story about Uxmal is that there was a witch who lived outside the Mayan temple of Uxmal and, though she had much power, she felt that she was unappreciated. She decided to have a child and make that child the ruler of Uxmal. She supposedly found a way, through witchcraft, to have a child born, not through her womb, but as an embryo of some kind, and hatched, much like a test-tube baby, you could say. The child learned the ways of his mother and was able to rise to the throne and become the ruler of Uxmal, much as the witch had planned. But when the dwarf became the king his mother, the witch, was not given the power she had wanted. He was a good and powerful ruler for a long time. He is thought of favorably by Mexicans and his legend, though hardly too believable, is not unlike many others from Mayan lore, and I am not embarrassed when they call me that name. I am proud of it.

I'm a short, stocky man. I have green eyes and a swarthy complexion. I am not dark-skinned like the true Mexican Indians, called Indios. There is no doubt that there is much Spanish blood in me and my fellow Mexicans know it and can see it in me, much like mulattos are seen in the United States.

I also have a large, almost rectangular shaped head, with high cheek-bones, a flat face and a flat head. I have read where the Mayans placed wooden boards on the heads of infants, thinking that by doing so they would shape the head in that way. They felt it was more suitable for carrying things on top of the head and that it was good to do so. There is no doubt that I have much Mayan blood in me, too. Matthew and David look like what they are, the products of a Lithuanian father and an Irish mother, and I am the product of the Spanish, Mayans and native Mexican Indios – a true Mestizo.

When I was with Matthew, before he got hurt, or David, it was like Mutt and Jeff. They towered over me, but that didn't bother me. I am proud of who I am. Matthew Sky and his brother, David, are the best friends I have in the world and I was always glad to be with them.

The other thing Matthew had learned to do since his injury, besides computers, was to play guitar. Before the injury, he hadn't ever played a musical instrument. While laid up for as long as he was, he taught himself how to play the guitar. His parents and Rebecca came to visit while I was there. By that time I knew the whole Sky family and I was welcome into any of their homes, anywhere, at any time. They didn't know until much later that I was an illegal immigrant, or an undocumented alien. I never told them or anyone about that for fear of getting them in trouble. A few days later, we all went into Cedar Key to a bar called the Rusty Rim and Matthew had his first public outing. They had a set of congo drums and I played along, though I hadn't ever played before. His sister sang, his parents danced and we had a good time. After a week in Cedar Key, David and I headed north.

I didn't drive very fast on the Interstate highways because I was afraid the Jetta wouldn't make it after the accident with the pig, but it did and David and I arrived in Block Island a few days later. He had found us a house where the rent wasn't too expensive and we each had our own separate room.

I never did get a driver's license in any state other than in Michigan. In Florida if you live there for more than ten days, you're supposed to get a Florida driver's license. I'm sure it was true in Rhode Island, too. I was always afraid of being caught and discovered…always, the whole time I was there. I heard of plenty of guys who got caught and sent back, but I never got caught. For over seventeen years I lived illegally in the U.S. with no problems at all.

I spent the summer on Block Island again and returned to Miami that fall. Between South Beach and Block Island, though I had little money, I was living a very enjoyable life. I always considered myself to be on a spiritual journey and kept God in my thoughts and prayers in my daily life. I thought often about the meaning and purpose of my life, what I was doing, where I had been and where I was going. Poems helped me to express my thoughts.

Reflections

We walk until we fall down;
We look back to see what made us fall;
We change, sometimes for the good and
sometimes not;
We choose between mountains and fields,
between sea and sky;
And then we come back to you, our God;
We are always with You, even when we don't
know it.

Chapter Eleven

Busted

The next year, 2005, I stayed longer than usual in Miami. My cousins were there and things were going on so it was mid- April before I was ready to head north. I was taking a bus to West Palm Beach to meet some friends who were going to drive me to Boston. I was planning to stay with Joy for a few days before going back out to Block Island. Things didn't really get started out there until the schools let out for summer but preparations began the first of May, which was when I was scheduled to start work at the Yacht Club.

The bus made many stops on its way from the Miami terminal to West Palm Beach. When the bus stopped at the Pembroke Pines station some people got off and others were waiting to get on, as was normal, but when I looked out the window I saw a dozen or more uniformed officers standing inside the station terminal. That was not normal. I immediately knew I was in trouble. The thought entered my mind that I had time to get off the bus and go the other way without being seen.

However, I was afraid that if they saw me leaving that would bring attention to myself and they might chase after me and then I would definitely be captured. I decided to stay put and hope for the best. Two of the officers boarded the bus and began questioning all of the passengers. They were all Customs and Immigration Officers in uniform. The others stood outside to question anyone who the two officers sent their way.

The bus was half full. I was the only Mexican but there were other

Latinos. There were mostly Anglos on the bus. Maybe it was a random search, but I didn't see them ask the Anglos any questions. I watched as they took a Latino woman and her two children from the front of the bus into custody. I kept my head down, pretending to be reading a book, hoping they wouldn't bother with me. No such luck.

The officer said it was a routine check and nothing to be concerned about. He first asked me if I was a citizen of the United States. I said no. He asked for identification and I gave him my Michigan driver's license. He turned to his fellow officers and said, "This one's got a driver's license!" He noticed that the license was dated in July of 2000 and he asked what I had been doing for the last five years. I told him that I had been traveling around, seeing the country, and that I'd been back and forth to Mexico.

He asked what I had been doing in Michigan and how I got a driver's license up there. I told him my brother lives in Michigan and is a U.S. Citizen and I stayed with him. He asked me if I had been working while in the United States and I told him that I was a writer and I wrote columns for newspapers in Mexico, which was true. He asked me how I paid for things. I told him my family supported me. He didn't believe me, or was suspicious at the very least, and told me that I had to get off the bus and talk to one of the other officers.

I told the other officer the same story but eventually I was handcuffed and put in a vehicle together with two other Latinos and taken to their headquarters somewhere nearby. I was placed in an interrogation room where the handcuffs were taken off and I sat there for hours until another man entered the room and began to ask me more questions.

I told him that I had entered the country legally, which was true, but I couldn't prove it, since I no longer had the passport from 1988 when I first entered the country and my visa had long since expired. I had renewed my passport In 2000 but the old passport had the stamps on it which would have proved that I entered legally. This passport showed an entry date of 2001 with nothing else. I told them that I had been issued a ten year visa, but that I had lost it

My Michigan driver's license was of great importance to them. As far as they were concerned, since it had an issue date of 2000 on it that proved that I'd been in the country for at least five years and since I had no visa, they assumed that I had been in the country all of that time. The driver's license was valid until 2008.

They didn't believe the part about the ten year visa and said visas are usually good for no more than six months. Besides, they told me, even if that was true, I wasn't allowed to work in the United States without a green card. Although I never admitted that I'd been working they knew that I couldn't have remained in the United States for five years without some sort of income. They said that was circumstantial evidence against me and that I would have to prove otherwise.

Later that day I was taken to the front desk and they handed me a Notice to Appear in a court in Miami the following week, after checking their records and determining that I hadn't been in any criminal trouble during the time I was in the United States. I was required to sign a bond. It read as follows:

IN THE UNITED STATES DISTRICT COURT
SOUTHERN DISTRICT OF FLORIDA

UNITED STATES OF AMERICA,
PLAINTIFF,

vs.

JORGE ALBERTO FRIAS-CASTILLO,
DEFENDANT

ORDER OF RELEASE ON RECOGNIZANCE

TO: JORGE ALBERTO FRIAS-CASTILLO
You have been arrested and placed in removal proceedings. In accordance with section 236 of the Immigration and Nationality Act and the applicable provisions of Title 8 of the Code of Federal Regulations, you are being released on your own recognizance provided you comply with the following conditions:

1. You must report for any hearing or interview as directed by the Immigration and Naturalization Service or the Executive Office for Immigration Review;

2. You must surrender for removal from the United States if so ordered;
3. You must not change your place of residence without first securing written permission from the officer listed above;
4. You must not violate any local, State or Federal laws or ordinances; and
5. You must assist the Immigration and Naturalization Service in obtaining any necessary travel documents.

FAILURE TO COMPLY WITH THE CONDITIONS OF THIS ORDER MAY RESULT IN REVOCATION OF YOUR RELEASE AND YOUR ARREST AND DETENTION BY THE IMMIGRATION AND NATURALIZATION SERVICE.

ROBERT GILMORE, SUPERVISOR
BORDER PATROL AGENT.

I, JORGE ALBERTO FRIAS-CASTILLO acknowledge that I have read the above, or had it explained to me in the Spanish language and that I understand the conditions of my release as set forth in this Order. I further understand that if I do not comply with these conditions, the Immigration and Naturalization Service may revoke my release without further notice.
Jorge Alfredo Frias-Castillo
I also received a Notice to Appear, which read:
IN THE UNITED STATES DISTRICT COURT
SOUTHERN DISTRICT OF FLORIDA

UNITED STATES OF AMERICA,
PLAINTIFF,

vs.

JORGE ALBERTO FRIAS-CASTILLO,
DEFENDANT

NOTICE TO APPEAR

In removal proceedings under Section 240 of the Immigration and Nationality Act
To: Jorge Alberto Frias-Castillo,
c/o US Immigration and Naturalization Services,
Krome Detention Center,
18201 SW 12th Street, Miami, FL 33194

You are hereby commanded to appear on April 21, 2005 at 9: a.m. in Courtroom 1, at the Krome Detention Center to answer to the charges that you are an alien present in the United States who has not been admitted or paroled. The Service alleges that you are

1. Not a citizen or national of the United States;
2. You are a native of Mexico and a citizen of Mexico;
3. You arrived in the United States at or near an unknown \ location on or about an unknown date and time; and
4. You were not then admitted or paroled after inspection by an Immigration Officer.

On the basis of the foregoing, it is charged that you are subject to removal from the United States pursuant to the following provisions of law: 212 (a)(6)(A))i) of the Immigration and Nationality Act, as amended, in that you are an alien present in the United States without being admitted or paroled, or who arrived in the United States at any time or place other than as designated by the Attorney General.

Representation: If you so choose, you may be represented in this proceeding, at no expense to the Government, by an attorney or other authorized individual authorized and qualified to represent persons before the Executive Office for Immigration Review, pursuant to 8 Code of Federal Regulations 3.16. Unless you so request, no hearing will be scheduled earlier than ten days from the date of this notice to allow you sufficient time to secure counsel. A list of qualified attorneys and organizations which may be able to represent you at no cost will be provided with this Notice.

YOU MUST NOTIFY THE IMMIGRATION COURT BY USING FORM EOIR-33 WHENEVER YOU CHANGE YOUR ADDRESS

OR TELEPHONE NUMBER DURING THE COURSE OF THIS PROCEEDING.

They told me that I was released and free to go. I didn't understand. They caught me, arrested me, handcuffed me and took me to jail, then they let me go. My friends told me that was a "Catch and Release" program. Many people never showed up after being arrested like I was and then let go. Maybe they went back to wherever they came from or maybe they just waited until they got caught again. I don't know. I thought about it but I felt that I deserved an opportunity to be allowed to stay in the country and I knew that if I didn't appear I probably would never be allowed to legally stay in the country.

I was ordered to appear in Court in Miami a week later. I went back to my Aunt's house and waited until the court date came. In the meantime, I talked to various people about what I should say or do. I didn't know if I should tell them that I had been in the United States for a long time or that I had just been there for a few months. I needed to talk to a lawyer but I didn't know any and wasn't able to pay for one. I decided to just show up and ask to speak to a lawyer and that's what I did.

The Federal Courthouse is in downtown Miami but my hearing was at the Krome Detention Center, located way out west on 182nd Avenue. I had a hard time getting there since little public transportation went that way, but I made it and I made my way through the metal detector and into the courtroom where about a hundred other people, just like me, were sitting. I listened to what the magistrate told the group and to what the people who went before me had to say. Most didn't speak English, or if they did, they didn't speak it well enough to be sure that they would understand what was being said to them, so most had an interpreter standing by their sides.

When it was my turn, before I said anything, the magistrate asked me if I was from Michigan, since I had given the officers who arrested me my Michigan Driver's License for identification. When I told him that I was, since that seemed like the right thing to say, he asked me if I wanted to have the venue of the case transferred to Michigan and I immediately said yes. I thought that was the smart thing to do. It would give me more time to figure things out. I asked the magistrate if I could speak to a lawyer and he told me to take care of it in Michigan. I was allowed to go free, again, but this time I was required to post a $500 cash bond, promising that I would appear in court in Detroit when notified of the hearing date.

When I returned from court, after having been released again, I went back to the bus station and bought a ticket for Rhode Island. My friends had already left for Boston. Besides, they didn't expect me to be released, and neither did I. They thought I'd be going to jail and told me I should just go with them and hope that I didn't get caught again. I thought long and hard about doing just that, but I didn't.

I had been caught and I was in trouble. I was in pain. I wrote a poem about how I felt.

Pain

How can I define the pain in my soul?
How can I describe the pain in my spirit?
How can I explain the trail on which I travel?
I trust my instinct to react appropriately to any radical
changes of the wind;
I trust that each new day will create a new world, a
better world than the day before;
I am a child of God, an angel of the earth
I fly in cities, on the seas and in forests
I see the souls of those who
suffer knowingly with troubled consciences, bothered by
who they are and what they do, unable to change;
I am an angel of God, one who lives day by day,
striving to help those who are around me,
and I am in pain and in trouble;
Lord, encourage me in this time of trouble and ease
the pain which I feel;
Lord, help me to encourage those who need
renewed hope, and
Lord, allow one of your angels to find and comfort me.

When back on Block Island I spoke to one of the members of the Yacht Club who was a lawyer about my problem, after asking him if he would promise to keep the conversation confidential. He had me give him twenty dollars and said that it was then an attorney-client privileged conversation. Because of that, he wouldn't tell anyone of it. When he found out my problem, he told me that he didn't handle immigration matters but he knew of an excellent law firm in Boston which did. He said they had offices in several cities and they specialized in such matters. He made a phone call and made arrangements for me to get an appointment to meet with one of the lawyers who he personally knew.

Chapter Twelve

Immigration Lawyers

A week later, on my day off, which was a Monday, I took the ferry to the mainland and then a bus to Boston. I found my way into the offices of the immigration lawyers and arrived at about noon. I brought all my papers with me, including my passport, which hadn't been taken from me. I guess they figured that if I wanted to use it to go back to Mexico that was alright with the U.S.

I met with a nice man, a few years older than me, and we discussed the case for about an hour. He told me that the fee would be $2500. I told him that I didn't have that much money right then, but that I was working and could have it saved up in a month or so. I didn't have to be in Detroit until September. He told me that would be fine. Whenever I had the money together I was to give him a call and I could come back in, sign a retainer agreement, and his firm would represent me.

A week later, I received the following letter in the mail:

IMMIGRATION LAWYERS, LLC
Boston, Massachusetts
April 29, 2005

Dear Jorge:

We are writing to follow-up on our meeting last week during which we discussed your options for remaining in the United States after your arrest and what to do about your scheduled hearing before an

Immigration Judge in Detroit in September. As we have explained, there are very few options for you to consider, and there are no guarantees in the outcome of any immigration matter that may be pursued. However, it is our opinion that you would benefit from attending the immigration hearing and defending yourself against the charges. We hope the following will provide some insight on your case.

The facts of your case are as follows: You claim you arrived in the United States over five years ago. At the time you first arrived you had a valid passport and a B-2 visitor visa stamped in the passport. However, sometime after arrival, you lost that passport, the visa contained therein, as well as Form I-94 Arrival/Departure record. You never reported this and never applied for a replacement of that visa. You did obtain and now have a new passport.

On April 14, 2005, you were stopped and arrested by an Immigration Agent in Florida. As a result of that arrest, you were briefly detained and released on your own recognizance. You first appeared in Court in Miami shortly thereafter. Following that hearing you were served with a Notice to Appear (NTA) before an Immigration Judge in Detroit, Michigan on September 13, 2005 at 9 a.m. The notice (NTA) states that you are to appear in court because you are "an alien in the United States who has not been admitted or paroled." Without providing documentation in the form of a valid passport with a visa, you were not able to prove that you entered the country legally.

Furthermore, you have remained in the United States well beyond the initial period of admittance on a tourist visa which was most likely a maximum of six months.

You appear ineligible for any type of relief such as cancellation of removal because you do not meet the criteria. For one, you would have to be able to prove that you have been continuously physically present in the United States for more than ten years, are of good moral character, have not been convicted of an offense, and can establish that removal would result in exceptional hardship to your U.S. Citizen spouse, parent or child. You do not appear to be able to meet those standards.

Therefore, since you have been served a Notice to Appear, you should plan to be at the place and time allotted on the NTA. If you were to leave the United States before appearing before an Immigration Judge, it is likely that your case would be placed on an "in absencia" status and therefore you would most likely be "ordered to be deported." Without a credible reason for not appearing, an order of deportation would be an unfavorable outcome for any possible future relief.

As discussed, we would be willing to represent you during this hearing and in order to make it more convenient for you, we would request a change of venue (change court location) to Boston, since you are now living in Rhode Island and Boston is the closest Federal Courthouse. That is for your convenience so that you will not be required to travel to Detroit. Please be advised that a change of venue is a discretionary matter and the Judge may not grant the request.

By attending the hearing, we may request, or the Immigration Judge may permit you to "voluntarily depart" from the United States at your own expense in lieu of being subject to removal/deportation proceedings. Agreeing to Voluntarily Depart" does not provide for any type of further proceedings or appeal process, though it may be a better option for you should any changes in the law occur in the future.

Because you have no criminal convictions or other related security concerns, it is likely that a Judge will grant you, or allow you, to voluntarily depart and that you will be released on your own recognizance until you leave the United States. The Judge may require you to post a voluntary departure bond. He will likely order your departure anytime within 120 days of the hearing (the maximum amount of time permitted to depart under current regulations). But it is unlikely that you will be detained or held in a detention center.

Given this scenario, we do have a few recommendations for you to consider before you appear before an Immigration Judge.

1. Request a change of venue to Boston;
2. Have affidavits in the form of letters from credible persons who are United States Citizens who can attest to your good moral character (we can help you draft those letters).
3. Submit an FOIA (Freedom of Information Act) request so that you will be able to see all of the documents the government has on you. It may take months for the information to be delivered, however, at least you can show the Judge that you are trying to prove that you entered the country legally 5 years ago; and have documentation that demonstrates you have the funds/money to

be able to post a bond (if required), manage the cost of living while in the United States before departure, and enough money to pay for a return trip to Mexico.

Finally, relief that may be available to you in the future is based on a bill pending in Congress called the "Secure American and Orderly Immigration Act of 2005" which addresses some of the serious issues with our current immigration system. Should this measure be passed, it could be of benefit to you, especially the Essential Worker Visa Program. While proposed Acts of such nature typically change greatly before becoming law, it is hard to say what kind of help this might be to your situation, if any. The following are the Terms and Conditions of this Agreement, should you wish to have us represent you in this matter:

Our legal fee will be $2,500.00 for preparation and processing prior to the hearing and attending the hearing with you in Boston, plus costs. Any time required in excess of this hearing and related matter will be charged on an hourly basis as follows: $225.00 per hour for the attorney and $150.00 per hour for the legal assistant assigned to your case to assist the attorney.

This legal fee is based in part upon our experience as to the amount of time required to accomplish your goals. In the event it appears that the time that we must expend to complete your case will substantially exceed this expected time, we would discuss a revision to this Fee Agreement with you.

Any service that you request in addition to the flat fee service will be subject to additional legal fees. Examples of services not included in the above basic legal fee are: appeals, reconsiderations, court review, waivers, extensions of nonimmigrant visas, new or amended applications based upon change in employment, immigration work for relatives not mentioned in this letter, non-immigration work and other services, including special services required due to unforeseen developments in your case or changes in the law.

In addition to legal fees, you are also responsible for costs, expenses and services such as government filing fees, express delivery and certified postage charges, toll telephone calls, advertising, photocopying, notary fees, translations and travel expenses. In some cases you will be asked to pay for those expenses directly. Where our law firm pays the expenses, we will ask you to reimburse us at the time those expenses are billed to you. You should feel free to ask us for an approximation of what the applicable costs in your case might be.

Termination of Attorney-Client Relationship-Our attorney-client relationship with you will be terminated upon our completion of the services outlined above. If you later retain us to perform services in connection with a new matter, out attorney-client relationship will begin again, subject to the Terms of Engagement as supplemented at that time. The firm reserves the right after termination of our attorney-client relationship to represent third parties in connection with matters that are, or may be construed to be, adverse to you so long as the matter does not involve the visa you are seeking or related immigration matters.

Consent- We would be pleased to discuss further any of the foregoing matters with you. If you decide to consent to our representation of you in connection with the Services consistent with our Terms of Engagement and in accordance with the understanding described above, please sign the enclosed copy of this letter in the place where indicated and return it to us.

Very truly yours.
Attorney-at-Law

When I had the money saved up, I called him back and made an appointment to meet with him again. When we met, I told him that I agreed to have the case transferred to Boston, since that would give me more time to stay in the United States and hope for the best. I formally retained the services of the Immigration Lawyers.

As he explained in the letter, the best thing I could hope for was that the Immigration Reform Act was passed and that a complete amnesty was declared for people like me who had been in the country for many years and hadn't caused any trouble. I hadn't committed any crimes, though I had definitely violated the terms of my admission to the U.S. by working and by over-staying my welcome. The ten year visa I had been given back in 1988 had long since expired. I had realized long ago that the visa I was given by the U.S. Consul who was a friend of one of my teachers at the college in Merida was a very unusual thing. I think they stopped giving visas for that long after that, if they ever did give out any others.

The government thought that I entered the country illegally because I didn't have my original Passport or the old visa. All they knew is that I was found in the country and they had no record of my entering the country, so therefore I must have entered illegally. Even if I had a passport from Mexico when I entered, as I told them, and I had renewed it as I did, that didn't prove that I had a visa which gave me a right to enter the United States.

So I had to try to figure out a way to prove that I had a valid visa when I entered but, as far as they were concerned, since I had been found in 2005 and I had a Michigan driver's license dating from 2000, they knew that I had been in the country since 2000, at the very least, that I had undoubtedly been working illegally, which was enough to get me deported, but they persisted with the argument that I had entered illegally also and that was one of the main allegations against me. I wanted to fight that.

If it would've kept me in the country, I could have obtained a copy of the visa issued to me way back in 1988, which was the only visa I ever had, except for the one Uncle Leo got for me, or maybe it was cousin Jenny, when I was fourteen and sixteen, but my lawyers said it wasn't going to make any difference. I would still be deported because no one would believe that I hadn't worked at all during those years.

For that matter, I could easily have obtained a copy of the Michigan license from 1989. However, my lawyers said it didn't matter that much if I could prove I entered legally because even if I did enter legally I wasn't allowed to work while here. I argued that unless they could prove that I had been working I should be allowed to stay. They said it made no difference because the circumstantial evidence was so strongly against me.

What I couldn't understand was why they never found any record of when I came into the country in Denver in 1988, or when I came in from Cuba that time in 1994, or from when I had the problem with Manny in Brownsville, or when Customs checked my papers, twice, when I came in with Francisco in Key West and then again in Miami. The only thing I could figure was that the government computers weren't as good back then as they are now. I would've thought that they were inter-connected and that the government had a file on Jorge Frias, from Progreso, Mexico, born in 1961, but they must not have.

I doubted that the American consulate in Merida had any records of the visa given me back in 1988 but I didn't even try to find out if they did or not because it didn't make a difference. What bothered me the most was that I was going to be ineligible to return to the United States for ten years. People who over-stayed their welcome were punished for ten years just the same as people who entered illegally. It seemed to me that one was worse than the other but my lawyers said that wasn't a valid argument to make and that it didn't matter. Maybe if I had more money to give them they would have been more willing to argue that I had entered legally but over-stayed my welcome.

Despite that, when I appeared in front of a judge I planned to tell him or her that I had entered legally on a visa issued to me by the U.S. Consulate in Merida when I originally entered the country.

Also, I was afraid to tell them too much. If I did, and told them all the places I had worked and all the people I had met or stayed with, that I could get those people in trouble. During all those years I never told anyone, other than family members and my lawyers, that I was illegally in the country for fear that I'd get them in trouble.

Unfortunately, nothing I ever told my lawyers seemed to work. They said the only thing they could do for me was delay the inevitable as long as possible and hope for a change in the law so that people who were illegally in the country for over five years and hadn't committed any crimes, like me, would be granted amnesty.

My attorneys, whose main office was in Boston, filed a request to transfer the case to Boston and it was granted. The hearing in Detroit in September was canceled. My attorneys told me that the issue of Mexicans coming illegally to the United States was one of great concern to the country and there was much consideration being given to declaring a complete amnesty to all such people, like me, who had lived in the U.S for over five years, as I had, provided they had not committed any crimes.

He said that the best thing they could do for me was drag the proceedings out for as long as they could and hope that the amnesty plan was made law. They also told me to pray that no illegal immigrants, like me, committed any horrendous crime anywhere in the United States or the plan would undoubtedly fail. They submitted a change of address form to the Immigration and Naturalization Service, or INS, giving them my address in Boston at the home of Joy Sky.

The lawyer explained that it would take some time to get all the paper work processed and I was free to come and go as I pleased, but that I had to make sure that they always knew how to get in touch with me. He explained that even if I was stopped by a law enforcement officer I wasn't in any trouble as all I needed to do was show them the bond I had signed, that I was involved with immigration proceedings, and that I was to appear in court at a later date.

He also said that I should carry those papers with me at all times, and I did. I still couldn't believe that I had been arrested for being in the country illegally yet I was now allowed to remain in the country on a $500 bond, on my promise to appear in court. I felt safer in the United States after being arrested than I did before being arrested. I was now legally in the country as an illegal alien. I called the lawyers office every month or so, just as he told me to, to check in and make sure I wasn't missing anything. They said the case could drag on for months while the government decided what to do about the immigration law and people like me.

Chapter Thirteen

The Public Debate

I read all that I could about what Congress was going to do about the immigration problem. Most of my information came from newspapers and television. In early May the following article appeared in the Boston Globe:

"McCain and Kennedy Sponsor Immigration Bill"

On May 12, 2005, the U.S. Senate announced a new immigration bill, entitled "The Secure America and Orderly Immigration Act of 2005" ("McCain-Kennedy Bill"). If signed into law by President Bush, this legislation would accord legal status to millions of undocumented workers and enable essential workers from foreign countries to enter the U.S. legally through employment with U.S. businesses.

Unlike other pending immigration bills, the McCain-Kennedy Bill has great promise of passing into law since it has support of both important Democratic and Republican Senators and House Representatives. This bill is sponsored by John McCain, a Republican senator, Edward Kennedy, a Democratic senator, Jeff Flake and Jim Kolbe, Republican representatives, and Luis Gutierrez a Democratic representative. The McCain-Kennedy Bill is similar to the "Guest Worker Program", a pending legislation supported by President Bush in 2004.

The important provisions of the McCain-Kennedy Bill are summarized below.

H-5A VISA-The McCain-Kennedy Bill would create a new non-immigration visa category for "essential workers" and for people with occupations needing few or no skills. The worker may maintain his/her status for three (3) years and extend his/her status for another three (3) years. The worker's family members (spouse and children under age of 21 years) may change and extend their non-immigrant status. This applies to people currently in the U.S. as well as outside the country. To qualify, the worker must not be seeking citizenship.

Unlike green card processing, H-5A visa processing is expected to take a fairly short period of time, which would be a matter of several months, rather than the usual several years for green card processing now required.

After obtaining an H-5A visa, the worker along with his/her family members may apply for green cards (i.e., U.S. permanent resident status). Alternatively, after four (4) years of H-5A status the worker may self-petition for green card processing.

H-5B VISA-The McCain-Kennedy Bill would create a new non-immigrant visa category for undocumented workers in the U.S. called an H-5B visa. It is a temporary visa for undocumented workers. The visa is for six (6) years. The undocumented worker's family members (spouse and children under age of 21 years) may change their status at the same time. When applying for a visa petition, the applicant must submit work history and must have clean criminal records. An H-5B holder may be authorized to work in the U.S. and travel outside of the U.S. The so-called "3-10 year bar" for illegal aliens leaving the U.S. and attempting to reenter the U.S. will not apply to the adjusted H-5B holders. An applicant older than 21 must pay a penalty of $1,000 to obtain an H-5B status. An H-5B visa holder may apply for permanent residency. The requirements for adjustment of status to permanent residency are the following:

(1) The applicant has been employed in the U.S. during the required period.
(2) The applicant pays a penalty of $1,000 (in addition to the $1,000 paid to get the H-5B visa).
(3) The applicant must submit a medical examination result.

(4) The applicant has paid all taxes during the requisite employment period.
(5) The applicant must be able to read and write ordinary English and have sufficient knowledge of U.S. history and civic matters.
(6) The applicant must pass a new criminal and security background check.
(7) The applicant has complied with draft registration requirements. Spouses and children are eligible to adjust to green card status with the principal application.

The immigration reform bill passed by the Senate that the House of Representatives takes up today would more than double the flow of legal immigration into the United States each year and dramatically lower the skill level of those immigrants. The number of extended family members that U.S. citizens or legal residents can bring into this country would double.

More dramatically, the number of workers and their immediate families could increase sevenfold if there are enough U.S. employers looking for cheap foreign labor. Another provision would grant humanitarian visas to any woman or orphaned child anywhere in the world at risk of harm because of age or sex.

I liked the sound of that. It seemed as if I might qualify for either of the two visas. There was a "path to citizenship" with the H-5B visa. I would be very happy if that bill passed.

However, a week later another article appeared which reflected the debate was still going on in Congress and was not over. The article read as follows:

HAGEL-MARTINEZ SEEK TO ALTER
MCCAIN-KENNEDY BILL

Legislation co-sponsored by Republican Sens. Chuck Hagel of Nebraska and Mel Martinez of Florida, which overcame some early stumbles now has bipartisan support in the Senate. The bill also has been praised by President Bush and he is expected to endorse it as a starting point for negotiations in his prime-time address to the nation tonight

All told, the Hagel-Martinez bill would increase the annual flow of legal immigrants into the U.S. to more than 2 million from roughly 1 million today, scholars and analysts say. These proposed increases are in addition to the estimated 10 million to 12 million illegal aliens already in the U.S. whom the bill would put on a path to citizenship. These figures also do not take into account the hundreds of thousands of additional immigrants who would be admitted to the U.S. each year under the guest-worker program that is part of the bill.

"Under this bill, if there is anyone left in the world, we would accept another 325,000 through the guest-worker program in the first year," said Rosemary Jenks, who opposes the bill and supports stricter immigration laws. The numbers have emerged only recently as opponents studied the hastily written 614-page bill in the five weeks since it was first proposed. It quickly stalled over Democratic refusal to allow consideration of any amendments to the bill, but debate resumes today after Senate leaders reached a compromise on the number of amendments.

"Immigration is already at historic levels," said Ms. Jenks. "This would double that at least."

The figures have been provided by Ms. Jenks by the Heritage Foundation. Several Senators who have steadfastly opposed the bill since it was proposed say that one of the most alarming aspects of the bill are the provisions that drastically alter not only how many but also which type of workers are ushered into the country.

Historically, the system that grants visas to workers has been slanted in favor of the highly educated and highly skilled. Currently, a little less than 60 percent of the 140,000 work visas granted each year are reserved for professors, engineers, doctors and others with "extraordinary abilities." Fewer than 10 percent are set aside for unskilled laborers. The idea has always been to draw the best and the brightest to America.

Under the Senate proposal, those priorities would be flipped. The percentage of work visas that would go to the highly educated or highly skilled would be cut in half to about 30 percent. The percentage of work visas that go to unskilled laborers would more than triple. In hard numbers for those categories, the highest skilled workers would be granted 135,000 visas annually, while the unskilled would be granted 150,000 annually.

What's more, opponents say the Hagel-Martinez bill would make it considerably easier for unskilled workers to remain here permanently while keeping hurdles in place for skilled workers. It would still require highly skilled workers who are here on a temporary basis to find an employer to "petition" for their permanent residency but it would allow unskilled laborers to "self-petition," meaning their employer would not have to guarantee their employment as a condition on staying.

"Slanting immigration law in favor of the unskilled and uneducated would be costly," said Robert Rector, a senior research fellow at the Heritage Foundation who has just completed a study on the impact of immigration and the new Senate bill. College-educated immigrants are likely to be strong contributors to the government's finances, with their taxes exceeding the government's costs," wrote Mr. Rector, who will release his findings today at a press conference with Sen. Jeff Sessions, Alabama Republican.

"By contrast, immigrants with low education levels are likely to be a fiscal drain on other taxpayers," he added. "This is important because half of all adult illegal immigrants in the U.S. have less than a high-school education. In addition, recent immigrants have high levels of out-of-wedlock childbearing, which increases welfare costs and poverty."

The flood of unskilled workers could cause other problems as well, opponents say. Because they would be allowed to "self-petition," their obtaining permanent residency here would bypass the Department of Labor, which currently monitors immigration to ensure that American workers are not displaced by foreign immigrant labor. But the greatest cost to the U.S. may not be the unskilled workers who immigrate here in the future, but the ones who are already here illegally.

Mr. Rector estimates that the Senate bill would grant citizenship to over 10 million illegal aliens. If allowed to become citizens, those immigrants would be permitted to bring their entire extended family, including any elderly parents. The long-term cost of government benefits to the parents of 10 million recipients of amnesty could be $30 billion per year or more," Mr. Rector said.

"In the long run, the Hagel-Martinez]bill, if enacted, would be the largest expansion of the welfare state in 35 years."

It was clear to me that opposition to the bill was mounting and both houses of Congress as well as the American public were having serious second thoughts about whether or not amnesty or a path to citizenship or any leniency to undocumented workers, like me, was appropriate. I hoped that either bill passed, though I preferred the McCain-Kennedy bill.

In the end, the version of the Immigration Reform Act passed into law as the Secure America and Orderly Immigration Act of 2005, signed by President Bush, did not contain a provision for amnesty or a path to citizenship. That was bad for me.

I called my lawyer and he told me what I already knew. At my request, he sent me a copy of the new law. It was sixteen pages long and I read every word, trying to find a way for me to stay in the U.S. (Author's Note: Please see Appendix A for a summary of the Act)

The Secure America and Orderly Immigration Act placed everything to do with immigration under the Department of Homeland Security, which was now responsible for securing the borders and preventing illegal immigration. It also provided for coordination of efforts between Mexico, Canada and other countries to combat illegal smuggling of human beings. It provided for incarceration of people who entered the U.S. illegally and it had provisions in it whereby the Federal government would pay states who incarcerated people like me who were illegally in the country. I didn't like the sound of any of that and failed to see how any of that was going to help me.

About half way into the bill, however, I began to see a few items that gave me some hope. I thought I might qualify as an "Essential Workers," but they were also called "non-immigrants," which I interpreted to mean those were people who were in the U.S. to work, not planning on becoming citizens.

This sounded to me like the old 'guest worker' programs of the Bracero days. Though I wanted more, I would have been happy with that, but I figured they were probably the migrants who worked in the fields. I hadn't done that kind of work, but I had been a landscaper. I wasn't interested in doing that kind of work, but if it would keep me in the country, I'd consider it. I'd have to ask my lawyers about whether or not I could qualify as an H-5A worker.

400,000 people would be admitted under that program and I liked the fact that it talked about making workers lawful permanent residents, not citizens, after four years, if they hadn't caused any trouble, of course.

I noticed where it said that jobs must first be advertized to American citizens and non-immmigrants, but I knew that most Americans wouldn't do the work Mexicans were willing to do to get into the U.S. I was interested in the part which spoke of workers who had been in the U.S. for over five years and had not been in any trouble being allowed to stay in the country.

The section that interested me the most, though, was Section 603 that spoke of aliens with extraordinary ability, or who were outstanding professors and researchers or multinational executives or managers. It also talked of advanced degrees, skilled workers and professionals, and it even mentioned unskilled labor that wasn't of a temporary or seasonal nature. I thought that since I was a college graduate and had management skills and other talents, like with photography, scuba diving, guide services, maybe even as a sailor, I didn't know…whatever it took, whatever talents I had, maybe one of them would work. I needed to talk to my lawyers and find out if any of those things might work.

Other than that, there were provisions in there to upgrade the technology so that information on a person trying to enter the country would be immediately accessible. From what I knew, that was a good idea, even though it would only hurt people like me. The fines for employers who employed illegals were to increase.

There were some protections for the workers and their families. One of the problems with the immigration situation is that if an illegal alien has a child in the United States the child is a citizen of the U.S. even though the parents are not. There were many people who didn't like that result. It made no difference to me as I had fathered no children, yet. How would that work? The parents have to leave but the child could stay behind? It was an unresolved problem.

The new Act wasn't anywhere near as helpful to people like me as the two other proposed bills would have been. My lawyers told me that they would do their best to convince the attorneys for the government that I should be allowed to stay in the United States under the terms of the new law, but they weren't all that confident that they could do that for me.

Chapter Fourteen

A Voluntary Departure

After the case was transferred to Boston the case was re-scheduled for May 16, 2006 in Boston. My lawyers explained that the government was dragging its feet on my case and on thousands upon thousands of cases like mine because it had been waiting to see if Congress was going to pass a comprehensive immigration reform act and, if so, what would be in it. Everyone—lawyers, judges and illegals alike – was waiting to see what that would be.

A week before the May hearing was to take place my attorneys called and informed me that the hearing was re-scheduled for August. A month later it was continued until November. Apparently the new law had created such an enormous back log of paper work that the government didn't have time to deal with me. While I was in Miami, making plans to return to Boston for the November 16 hearing, they called to tell me that it was continued again to May 5, 2007.

Ironically. It was on May 5, 1862 that the French were defeated in a battle outside of the city of Puebla at the hands of the city's Militia. Although immediately following the defeat Napoleon then sent 30,000 troops to capture Puebla and later capture Mexico City and control the entire country, the loss at Puebla was a monumental defeat for the French Army. Mexico celebrated the victory and still does, as does the entire world nowadays.

France later withdrew all of its forces within the next five years. Some say that the United States provided aid to Mexico at that time, after its own Civil War ended. Mexico and the United States have a long and tortured history together, but there were times of mutual respect and cooperation, too.

Cinco de Mayo is now celebrated all across Mexico and the United States and all over the world wherever Mexicans can be found. I was hoping maybe I'd have a reason to celebrate Cinco de Mayo in 2007, but it didn't look like that was going to happen.

I spent that winter in Miami. I worked at the Sagamore Restaurant, one of the nicer restaurants in South Beach, as a waiter. It was located at the corner of Collins Avenue and 18th Street. I didn't know it at the time, but that would be my last winter season in Miami.

In March of 2007 I traveled out to Oregon, where Matthew Sky had moved so that he could be out of the hot, Florida summer sun. Hot weather wasn't good for him and caused him to develop sores that sometimes took weeks to heal. He needed to be in a colder climate, especially during the summer.

He had bought a house in Eastern Oregon in a little town called Baker. It wasn't too far from what was called the Oregon Alps and Joseph, Oregon. That was a beautiful area, with a huge lake surrounded by mountains, where Chief Joseph and his tribe were allowed to live on a reservation, after their home lands were taken from them.

We fished for salmon and trout in the rivers and streams and caught many rainbows in the mountain lakes. Matthew played music at a few of the local bars and we had a good time together. We also did some traveling.

I took many photographs of the area. Matthew drove me all around the state and down as far south as Reno, Nevada where Matthew's sister, Amy, lived. We stayed with her for a while and camped at Yosemite and in the Redwood Forest.

I did some writing during that time, too. It was a melancholy time for me as I knew what awaited me. A week before the hearing date, I left Matthew and went back to Boston to face the music. It looked like the hearing set for May 5, 2007 might actually take place.

I met with my lawyers on May 4, the day before I was to appear in Court, though I thought long and hard about not doing so. Finally, over two years after I had been arrested, the case was going to come to trial. I had obtained over 50 letters of recommendation from many people of substance and good standing to present to the Court, even though I was told it would do no good at that point.

The lawyers said that I could have asked for a formal hearing and required the government to call witnesses and present evidence to prove its case. That would have delayed my departure even longer, but we would have lost, for sure. The risk was that I would be involuntarily deported, which would make it that much harder for me to get back to the United States, if ever. I also knew that I could still run and maybe never be discovered, as I had done for most of my life. It had been almost twenty years that I had been in the United States, working, causing no trouble and having no problems. It was time to go back to Mexico and be with my parents.

I talked to my lawyers at great length. Unfortunately, they had found no way that I could win the deportation hearing. They told me that the government wanted me out of the country and wouldn't compromise their position at all. In fact, they were upset by the amount of time that had passed since I had been arrested, which was understandable.

After talking to them, I agreed to voluntarily depart the country. They notified the government lawyers and a deal was arranged. I would still have to appear in court, as scheduled, but the government would announce that no trial was to take place as I was going to voluntarily depart. They agreed to allow me some additional time to do so.

Of all the letters of recommendation I submitted, and there were many good ones, ones that made me feel proud and made me want to cry. The one I liked the best came from the Commodore of the Yacht Club. It was dated September 25, 2004. The man who wrote it did so in case I needed it for another job. He had no idea that I was an illegal alien. He just liked me. I didn't even ask him for a letter of recommendation. It read as follows:

"For the past several years Jorge Frias has been an employee of the Yacht Club doing repair of our facilities and other maintenance work. Shortly after beginning work here, due to his knowledge of sailing and sailboat maintenance, he was promoted and became a Marina Assistant. Shortly after receiving that promotion, due to his excellent social skills and admirable work ethic, he took over as our Junior Sailing Program

Coordinator. He was entrusted with the lives of the children of our members, many of whom are quite prominent in the community.

Mr. Frias is a goodwill ambassador for his native country of Mexico. While working here, under my direct supervision, he was responsible at times for the management of approximately fifty personnel. His primary obligation was to keep 650 members happy and satisfied, which he did in outstanding fashion.

I consider him to be in the top one percent of our work force. He is a reliable and dependable worker and I have no hesitancy in recommending him to you as a prospective employee, no matter what the job entails."

The Judge looked at the attorney representing the government and asked, "Why do I have to deport this man? Why can't you round up the drug dealers and criminals and let me deport them?"

He looked at me and said, "Mr. Frias, I wish there was something I could do to help you, but there isn't. I am bound to follow the law and the law requires that you leave the country. I will allow you to voluntarily depart and I will give you plenty of time to do so, but you must depart. I wish you good luck."

The Order required me to leave by June 6. It read as follows:

UNITED STATES IMMIGRATION COURT
JOHN F. KENNEDY BUILDING, ROOM 320
BOSTON, MASSACHUSETTS, 02203-0002

IN THE REMOVAL CASE OF
FRIAS-CASTILLO, JORGE ALBERTO
ORDER

This is a memorandum of the Court's Decision and Orders entered on May 5, 2007. This memorandum is solely for the convenience of the parties. The oral or written findings, Decision and Orders are the official opinion in this case.

Respondent's application for voluntary departure was GRANTED until June 6, 2007, upon posting a voluntary departure bond in the amount of $500.00 to the INS within five business days from the date of this Order, with an alternate Order of removal to Mexico. Respondent shall present to the INS within fifteen (15) days from the date of this Order all necessary travel documents for voluntary departure.

Respondent was orally advised of the LIMITATION on discretionary relief and the consequences for failure to depart when and as required.

If you fail to voluntarily depart when and as required you shall be subject to a civil money penalty of at least $1,000, but not more than $3,000, and be ineligible for a period of ten (10) years for any further relief under INA sanctions 2408, 245, and 246 (INA Section 2408 (d);

If you are under a final order of removal and if 1) you willfully fail or refuse to depart when and as required, 2) make timely application in good faith for any documents necessary for departure, or 3) present yourself for removal at the time and place required, or, if you conspire to or take any action designed to prevent or hamper your departure, you shall be subject to civil money penalty of up to $500 for each day under such violation. (INA Section 2740 (a). If you are removable pursuant to INA 237 (a) then you shall further be fined and/or imprisoned for up to ten (10) years. (INA Section 243 (a)(1).

Date: May 7, 2007 Francis L. Cramer, Judge
Appeal waived by Respondent.

Again, I was required to post a bond in the amount of $500 but again, I was allowed to walk out of the courtroom and travel about as I pleased. I stayed at Joy's house most of the time. While there, I received the following letter from my attorney:

IMMIGRATION LAWYERS, LLP
One Harvard Square
Boston, Massachusetts

May 8, 2007
To: JORGE FRIAS CASTILLO
Re: Voluntary Departure Order
Dear Jorge:

This letter is provided as a follow-up to our meeting and your court appearance on May 5, 2007. As you told Judge Cramer, you elected to voluntarily depart the United States within 30 days of May 5, 2007. We present this information to you for your consideration.

As you heard, Judge Cramer ordered Voluntary Departure in your case. You are required to leave the United States no later than June 6, 2007. The reason for this is because you violated the terms of your non-immigrant status by staying much longer than permitted. Furthermore, while you claim that you entered the United States legally in B-2 status, the government believes that you entered illegally, without documentation (undocumented). We have exhausted all available options for you to remain in the United States. Alternative immigration benefits are also not available at this time. Under Voluntary Departure rules, no appeals are permitted.

Therefore, you should depart the United States no later than June 6, 2007. If you stay beyond this date, Immigration and Customs Enforcement (ICE) will likely find you, hold you in custody and deport you. It is a serious offense to remain in the United States beyond the Voluntary Departure period. You may be subject to civil penalties of $1,000 to $5,000, and will be ineligible to apply for virtually any other form of relief while in the U.S. for 10 years.

Voluntary Departure is considered a form of relief because it is granted at the outset of a hearing and you are not ORDERED to be removed or deported. However, a grant of Voluntary Departure does not cure the 10 year bars to re-entering the United States under United States Code 1182 (a) (9) (B). A person who overstays their period of authorized status for more than 180 days (6 months) is automatically barred from returning to the United States for a period of three years. A person who overstays their visa status for more than one year, as you have done, is automatically barred from re-entering the United States for 10 years.

Because there are no forms of relief available to you, Voluntary Departure is the most reasonable solution. As present regulations stand, you are subject to a 10 year bar from legally returning to the United States. However, if new immigration legislation is passed by Congress, and depending on what is written into the regulation, you may become eligible for future benefits.

If you were to marry a United States citizen or U.S. permanent resident, you may also be eligible for an additional form of relief. We could file a waiver of inadmissibility to address the issue of the ten year bar from your return to the United States, and then process you for permanent resident status through Consular Processing.

After you arrive in Mexico, you should visit the nearest U.S. Consulate and complete paperwork (Form G-146) so that the government is assured that you have returned to Mexico under Voluntary Departure, as ordered. This form will be forwarded to the Immigration Service in the U.S. It will also facilitate the release of your $500 bond.

Jorge, it has been a pleasure representing you in this matter and we want to stay in contact with you. We will keep your family's address on file and please let us know if you relocate. We will also inform you by e-mail should legislation be enacted that may benefit you.

Please contact us should you have any questions regarding this letter. For now, we wish you all the best on your return to Mexico.

Very truly yours,
Immigration Professional

I was making plans to depart as ordered and saying good bye to all of the many friends I had made in Boston, Newport and on Block Island. Most were surprised to hear about what had happened to me. All were disappointed to learn that I'd be leaving. I invited everyone to come visit me in Progreso.

I had asked my lawyers if I could have some more time to go. My lawyers asked the court to give me additional time to go. I don't know what reason they gave but I received a letter telling me that my request for an extension of time to depart from the United States was approved and that I had until August 20, 2007 to depart.

There were no more appeals left, no more requests for extensions of time, no more laws to be passed, amnesty was not going to be granted to illegal immigrants, or aliens. I had to go. I was very sad about what had happened to my great journey. It was as if I had been flying like an eagle with the wind and was shot down.

When the day for departure came, both Joy and Mary Sky took me to the airport in Boston. I boarded a plane headed for Cancun, with a stop-over in Philadelphia. It was to be about a six hour trip.

On the flight back I was sad, but I reflected on all the things I had done. I remembered the day in Seattle when I was sitting at a coffee shop on Alaskan Avenue, overlooking Puget Sound with some of the guys I was working with. We were talking about places we had been. One of the guys had looked at me and said "Hey, man! I've never been outside of Spokane County. How is it that you, a Mexican laborer, can have gone all over the country?" It was true. I had been all over America, admiring the beauty of America, making friends along the way. It had been a great journey and I hated to see it end. I had been like a caballero, riding alone.

I had followed my heart, followed the wind, and come to a dead-end. I wrote another poem.

New Beginnings

I return to where I began;
Though I have experienced a great adventure, my heart is the same;
My mind, my body, my arms, and my legs have met all the challenges;
I recall the eyes of people who viewed me with honor and respect;
I will carry on with energy and peace and continue to search for meaning in my life;
I will always see beauty in flowers and blue skies;
I will continue to smell the perfume of forests;
I will walk in the clouds and ride the waves of the seas;
I will travel through time with memories of yesterday, and though those days are gone, never to be again, I will always keep them in my heart and my soul;

Chapter Fifteen

Back in Mexico

When I got back to Mexico, I went home to be with my parents. I came back with little more than I left with, and I was almost twenty years older. It had been September of 1988 when I left and it was now late August of 2007. I had made many friends in the United States, the best of which were Matt Sky and his family. A few women who I confided with had offered to marry me so as to make me "legal," but I wanted to marry for love, and though I loved all of them, it was not in the way I had loved Mary or Rayna. I couldn't do that, though now I found myself wishing that I had.

I had been many places and seen many things from the far northwest of the United States, to the New England states in the northeast, down to Florida and Key West in the southeast and to California in the southwest part of the country. I had been to the "big" cities of Chicago, Detroit, Boston, New York, Washington, D.C., Miami, Dallas, Houston, and Baltimore, among others. I had hiked and camped in the Rocky Mountains, the Appalachian Mountains, Glacier National Park, the Blue Ridge Mountains and many others.

I had fished in the Everglades and in the mountains of Oregon, Montana, and the Lakes of Michigan. I had wind-surfed in Chesapeake Bay. I had swum in the Colorado River, the Potomac, the Columbia River, the Snake and many others. I had fished in the Gulf of Mexico off of Cedar Key. I had seen much and done much, though there was much I had yet to see and yet to do. More than anything else, though, I missed the people.

The United States, unlike Mexico, Spain, France, China or anyplace else in the world, was full of people like me…people who wanted to travel, explore places and do things. Many were recent immigrants to the country, while many more were second, or third generation immigrants. I didn't talk to people about this too much because, as an illegal person, it wasn't something that I wanted people to know about, but it was rare to find anyone whose family had lived in the United States for more a couple of generations.

America is a country full of immigrants, though those who had been here for only a few generations sometimes seemed, to me, to feel as if they "belonged" and we did not. To me, the part that was hardest to understand was that for many years Mexicans were welcomed into the United States and there was no border patrol. Mexicans could come and go as they pleased, much like Americans don't need a visa to travel to Mexico or Canada today.

It took a long time for me to adjust to being back in Mexico. The reality set in that I wasn't going to be able to return to the United States for ten years and I didn't like that. There were friends I wanted to see that I could not. I thought about just going back as I had so many times before, but I knew that this time if I was caught I would probably be put in jail. Despite that, I think about it, knowing that I shouldn't do it. I wrote a poem about how I was feeling.

Survival

The plight of man is to endlessly seek survival;
I, like all men, toil between the time frame of
years between my birth and my death;
God works in an eternity;
Man seeks the truth known only by God;
It is a journey every man travels alone;
However, God is with us and never will He abandon us;
I know that the hour of truth gets closer for me every day;
I face the daily challenges and I embrace them;
They touch me and they test me;
I make footprints in the air and on the wind;

I live in a world of childhood without being a child.
I always look for ways to strengthen my soul;
I treasure that which is mine and thank God for what I have been given;
I follow the light, for HE is the light of the world;
I fight against darkness, for that is the domain of evil;
Man will survive, though I will not.

After I was home for a few weeks I received the following letter from the United States government.

U.S. DEPARTMENT OF JUSTICE
IMMIGRATION AND NATURALIZATION SERVICE
IMMIGRATION AND CUSTOMS ENFORCEMENT
200 DYER STREET
PROVIDENCE, RI 02903

The records of this office show that permission was granted to JORGE FRIAS CASTILLO to remain in this country until August 20, 2007. This office has no record of departure from the United States.

To assist in the completion of our records relating to the departure of aliens, you are requested to complete the back of this form and

(1) Return it in the attached self-addressed envelope.
No postage is required if mailed anywhere in the
United States; and (2) Mail or take it to the office
of the nearest American Consul and ask him/her
to return it to this office.

Please select and complete the statement below which most accurately reflects your knowledge of this individual. The person inquired about: JORGE FRIAS:

(1) Departed from the United States at _____ (port of departure) on _____ (date) via _____ (name of vessel or other means of transportation.
Supervisor

I went to the U.S. Consulate in Merida and wrote the last chapter of my odyssey.

I was resigned to live in Progreso for years to come. I kept asking myself why I couldn't be happy living in Progreso. My father has lived his entire life there, never wandering, never straying too far from his home. He is happy there. He loves his wife, his family, his work, his community, the Yucatan and his country. Why couldn't things be that simple for me?

I was born and raised in Progreso. My grandfather, Sixto Frias, moved his family, my family, from Sisal to Progreso in 1910, during the days of the Revolution, when Pancho Villa led thousands of men on horseback all across the country, capturing cities on the way in the north of Mexico. In the south, Evelio Zapata preached land and liberty for the common man, the paisanos, not just the rich and especially not the rich foreigners. Pancho Villa and Zapata joined together to bring about a change in Mexico and my family was a part of it.

My family's home was located directly across from the Plaza of the town of Progreso, which consists of about a quarter mile square in the middle of the city. The church that my family attends is across the street, as is a well-known Café, called the Cordobez Café, named after a famous bull-fighter. City Hall, called Palacio Municipales, a bank, some other city buildings, and a school named Candelaria where all of my family attended, including my father, were on the square, too.

My grandfather prospered in Progreso. He started at least four newspapers and became one of the leading journalists in the area. My father worked with him and followed in his footsteps, carrying on the tradition. My father was born in Progreso. He is an author, too. He wrote over a dozen books about the history of Progreso and the Yucatan, the most significant of which is entitled Monografia Historica Geografica, Maritiima Y Cultural del Puerto de Progreso de Castro Yucatan. It is considered one of the leading historical accounts of the area and is now considered a national treasure.

Sixto moved to Progreso from Sisal because the commercial business in the Peninsula had increased dramatically at the end of the 19th century as ports on the Gulf of Mexico had become much more attractive to the world economy, but Sisal had been left behind. He saw that his future was in Progreso and he was correct. At the turn of the century Cuba and Spain were at War with the United States after the sinking of the U.S. Maine in the harbor of Havana in 1898 shifted traffic away from Cuba and to Mexico and the Yucatan. As a result, many of the harbors in the Gulf were found to be too small and not safe for commercial traffic. Ports were either enlarged or other ports were created. Progreso was one of the ports which was created to meet the increased demand.

My grandfather had been there as the area grew. More and more products from the Yucatan were being demanded by the rest of the world, products such as palo de tinte, which is sap from a tree from which ink was derived. It was much sought after at the time. The sap was black and it was used in Europe and the United States for inkwells and paint. The horizons of Progreso and the Yucatan were expanding.

Exploration of the Yucatan by foreigners other than the Spanish began in the late 1830s when a prominent New York attorney, John Lloyd Stephens, accompanied by an artist named Frederick Catherwood, traveled extensively throughout the region, focusing their efforts on finding ancient ruins in the jungles. Catherwood drew sketches of all that he saw and, together with Stephens, they wrote and published a book entitled *Incidents of Travel in Central America, Chiapas and the Yucatan*. It was received with wild enthusiasm in Europe and the United States and went through ten printings in less than three months.

Gradually, more and more visitors came to the area and much commercial use for the native plants and trees was discovered. One of the most important of the explorers to the area was a man named Adams who, in the late 1800s, discovered that the sap of the Zapote tree could be used as chewing gum. The word "chiclets" is a Mayan word meaning 'chic-mouth-move' because the Mayans put the sap in their mouths and chewed on it. That was the beginning of a previously unknown and unheard of industry in the United States and around the world. The Wrigleys in Chicago were the ones who benefitted the most from those chiclets.

Meats, salads, fish, fruit and other products became sought after by the outside world as well. Fish such as Pompano and Snook were in particularly high demand. Henequen, which is like the tequila plant, was used to make thick and heavy ropes and fibers which were used for ships and other things.

But it was the maize, or the corn crop, which is said to have been the primary contribution of the area to world commerce. The Mayans developed an agricultural system that was a marvel to the world, and it was based upon the maize crop. Some say it is the most significant contribution to the world economy made by the Mayans, even more so than their accomplishments with astronomy and mathematics.

Not only was there a much increased amount of exportation taking place, but there was also a greatly increased amount of importation occurring as well. Direct commerce with various countries around the world, instead of through Spain and Cuba only, brought items such as hardware, nails, wire, linen and a great variety of other goods from countries around the world to the Yucatan. Commerce with other countries increased dramatically and it was no longer dominated by the Spanish.

During the early 1800s, the only ports for the dispatch of goods on the Yucatan peninsula were Campeche, Sisal and Bacalar, which is now in Belize. England took control over Belize during the middle of the century. Tampico and Vera Cruz were the main eastern ports for most of the country, but not for the Yucatan. Sisal was the closest point to the city of Merida which was and still is the biggest city in the Yucatan, having become a city 1542, but Sisal was a good distance from Merida and the roads were poor and the harbor was shallow.

The government wanted to find a faster entrance to the seas, closer to Merida. The shallow waters of the harbor in Sisal were becoming a problem for the increasingly larger commercial ships, too. In 1840, Mr. Juan Miguel Castro Martin, a visionary and a lover of the Yucatan, together with others, sought to find a port better than Sisal for Merida.

At the furthest western point of the Yucatan Peninsula he found an undeveloped area with beautiful white beaches, grapes and dunes which seemed to him to be much closer to Merida. That area was where he decided the new port should be built. It was only 20 miles from Merida, much closer than Sisal.

They named the area Progreso. From that day forward the town of Progreso went from being an idea to a reality. The Mexican government began creating a road between Merida and Progreso. Once the road was finished, Mr. Castro convinced the government to move the Customs

Office from Sisal to Progreso. Once that occurred, Sisal's fate was sealed, as was Progreso's.

By 1846, the year the Mexican-American War began, Progreso had become the biggest and best port in all of the Yucatan. In 1856, the president formally authorized the creation of the town and streets and lots were plotted for sale to the public. The first house was built with palm fronds on the roof and mud, wood and stone in the walls. The town began to grow. On May 20 of 1866, Juan Miguel Castro convinced the government to create a railroad from Progreso to Merida, the capital of the state of Yucatan.

In 1870 the government began building a large pier to accommodate bigger ships. Ships bringing products either to or from the Yucatan had to go through Progreso. The first ships from New York and Havana came to Progreso in 1871.

The first telegraph line was established in Progreso in1871. Mail service was established by horse and carriage a few days per week. The first school opened in 1872. In January of 1875, a city hall was erected. In 1875, street lights with candles as light were installed. In 1881 that railroad service began.

The first newspaper called El Faro, which means the lighthouse, was produced by Domingo canto Moreno. He created a weekly magazine called El Horizonte, as well. Chiuxulub, a ship capable of crossing the Atlantic Ocean, anchored off of Progreso in 1886. In February of 1893 the first baseball game between teams from Progreso and Merida was played. The Plaza Park was opened in 1899 by the governor of Yucatan.

The Lighthouse was opened with a range of 17 miles before the end of the century and the port had four piers. So many ships from all over the world were coming to Progreso that it was not unusual to see them anchored offshore, waiting to dock. The warehouses were insufficient to accommodate all of the merchandise that was coming and going. In 1912 the first plane landed in Progreso. It was a hydro plane, landing on the water. It flew at 95 miles per hour.

By the turn of the century 5,431 people lived in Progreso. There was much optimism for the city at the turn of the century. It was during this period of economic growth and prosperity that Sixto Frias moved to Progreso. He saw the need for pamphlets, stationary and other things to accomodate the needs of businesses in the area, plus postcards and brochures for tourism, and newspapers and magazines, all of which developed slowly over time, but Progreso, true to its name, was the most progressive part of the country, at least on the Gulf side, for tourism and commerce alike. It was an exciting time for him and he was at the center of what was taking place in the area.

At that time, only the rich and most adventurous of tourists came to the Yucatan, but my grandfather saw that it was the beginning of something much bigger than anything the Yucatan had ever seen before. He was a visionary. He also had the courage to act on his visions. I am a beneficiary of that courage.

It was probably a good time to be as far away from the turmoil the rest of the country was in. too. He wasn't able to avoid the carnage, however. In 1914, 150 rebels captured the palace in Progreso and murdered the mayor of the town. In 1915 a Mexican warship exploded when it collided with a canoe which contained a barrel of dynamite in Progreso's harbor. Thirty people died. The entire country was at war.

In the 1920s, as some degree of normalcy was being restored, the development of Progreso continued. In 1936 a new pier, made of concrete, was begun. It was said to be the largest pier in the world. It opened in 1947. The roads and railroads were being improved all over the country, not just in the Yucatan. Merchandise began flowing more easily to and from Progreso and throughout the entire country.

Since fishing had become a more popular industry both for commercial fisherman and tourists, in June of 1968, President Gustavo dias Ordaz opened a new port called the Port of the Fishermen. More boat traffic flowed in. President Luis Echevaria Alvarez created a Free Trade Zone in Progreso in 1970. Progreso remained a principal port for the state of Yucatan and for Mexico at that time. That was the high-water mark for the city.

In that year, 1970, the President of Mexico invested millions and millions of dollars to develop an area in the Yucatan where primarily American businesses could spend billions of dollars to construct enormous resort hotels and attract hundreds of thousands of tourists annually. There were no cities or towns there before. It had been all jungle, much like Progreso had been in the mid-1800s.

The islands of Cozumel and Isla de Mujeres had been a destination for cruise ships full of tourists for years, and there were small cities and towns along the coastline, but nothing to compare with what Cancun would become. In the mid-1970s, when Cancun opened for business, it was the beginning of the end of Progreso. Playa del Carmen came into existence not long after to help seal Progreso's fate.

Once Hilton, the Ritz-Carlton and others began to offer truly elegant accommodations for those seeking an alternative to the glitz and glamour of Miami Beach, Progreso was doomed. When, in 1960, the revolution led by Fidel Castro successfully overthrew the dictator, Battista, Havana and the beaches of Cuba were no longer open to foreigners, especially Americans. Multitudes of visitors thronged to the west coast of the Yucatan Peninsula, leaving Progreso to shrink like fruit on a vine which had been severed from its tap root.

For almost 100 years, my grandfather and my father operated newspapers in the Yucatan. My father's books on the history of the Yucatan were labors of love and are now kept in the official archives of the Mexican government. He published them himself on a small printing press he bought with his own money and operated out of his house. For decades, few people bought the books and he had trouble giving them away.

It wasn't until the late1990s when the Mexican government and some people in the academic world took notice of the merit and volume of my father's work that he began to get some recognition, and some money. I recall the day when a man came to the door of our house asking for a copy of his first history book. My father told him that he had no copies and that it was long out of print. Not long after, the Mexican government authorized the re-printing of that book and several others. It sold out immediately, as did a second printing.

After sixty years of labor, my father began to see a profit from his labor. It was long after I was out of the house. My father is ninety years old now. My mother, Irma Castillo, who is from the city of Villahermosa in the state of Tabasco, Mexico, is ten years younger. They remain in love with one another. His main pleasure in life is to walk out the front door to his home, into the plaza, have a cup of coffee with friends, sit and talk, which he does every day. He still writes, too. He is always writing. Even at ninety, he continues to write. My mother's passion is caring for him and her family, including me.

Another of his pleasures is to sit in front of a TV on a Sunday afternoon and watch the bullfights from "La Corrida de los Toros" in Mexico City. Though there are bullfights in Merida most Sundays during the summer months, and many of the smaller towns throughout the Yucatan have bullfights on a regular basis, it is the ring in Mexico City that is the "major league" of Mexican sport. Barbaric as they are, the tradition of bullfights is deep within the fabric of Mexican culture.

As ships, and later airplanes, brought the outside world to the Yucatan, businesses which provided access to the magnificent remnants of the once mighty Mayan empire sprang up, as did the hotels, motels, restaurants, tour buses, taxis, gift shops and all the rest. Unfortunately for Progreso, those businesses sprung up in Cancun and Playa del Carmen. Progreso was a town in the midst of a deep decline.

I can still walk on Progreso's beautiful beach, though I cannot do anything more than admire from a distance the port where cruise ships come several times a week. Pedestrians are not allowed on the pier. Progreso is not what it was during its golden years and it will take an enormous infusion of cash for it to compete with its neighbors to the east. By the time I was a teenager, I knew that Progreso was not progressive enough for me. I would have to leave. Nothing had happened to change that. If anything, the intervening years only convinced me of it all the more.

After a few weeks, I went back to Cancun, looking to start guiding again, doing the things I had done since I was a teenager. I didn't have any trouble finding a job. There weren't too many people who could speak English fluently, as I had learned to do, and even fewer who could speak Italian and French, too. More and more people were coming from Italy and France, and other places in Europe. More and more Asians were coming to the Yucatan, too. Fortunately, most of them know how to speak English, many of whom having been educated in the United States. I thought to myself that maybe I should try to get into the country as a student. I wanted to be in America, not in Progreso, but that was no longer an option.

Chapter Sixteen

CANADA AND RAYNA

After I had settled in and was feeling a little better about myself, I made contact with Rayna. She was glad to hear from me and, even though she had a boyfriend and was thinking of getting married, we started communicating with each other. Several months later, she broke up with her fiance' and we made plans for me to go visit her.

I still had a valid passport and Mexicans didn't need a visa to get into Canada. I purchased a ticket. Rayna found a job for me and wrote a letter saying that I would be staying with her and her family. The days passed slowly as I waited impatiently for the day I would be leaving on another adventure.

The day finally arrived and I boarded an Aero-Mexico plane for the United States and then on to Canada. We stopped in Houston, and then Denver, before getting to Alberta, but I didn't have to go through customs at any of those cities as we either stayed on the plane or in an area right outside the gate. Once I arrived in Alberta, I was taken into a separate room by a young Canadian Customs Officer who proceeded to grill me.

Little did I know that two days before I arrived Canada had passed a law requiring people from Mexico to obtain visas. I had known that the northern border of the United States was a whole lot easier to cross than the southern border and apparently the United States had convinced the Canadian government to do something to prevent Mexicans from getting into the United States from their country.

The man asked me how much money I had. I was carrying $2,000 and I told him so. He asked how long I planned to stay and I told him that I didn't know. I was visiting friends and would be traveling with them. I showed him the letter from Rayna saying as much. He asked if I planned to work and I told him that I didn't. He kept saying that I didn't have enough money for an extended stay in Canada. I told him that I would leave when my money ran out. That didn't satisfy him.

At one point, I agreed with him and said, "Okay, I'll agree to stay for a week, or two, whatever you say, and then leave. How's that?" But he wouldn't allow me to do that either. I asked why I couldn't just be a visitor to the country, even for a few days, just to go shopping and see a few friends, but he wouldn't answer.

I asked if he would allow me to see Rayna and he refused. I asked if I could talk to Rayna on the phone and he refused. I'm sure he had information through his computer that revealed my history with the U.S. because it soon became apparent that he wasn't going to let me in the country.

Finally, he reluctantly allowed me to call Rayna to tell her that I wasn't going to be allowed into the country. She knew an immigration lawyer and gave me his name and number. The Customs Officer allowed me to call him.

When I told him the problem, the lawyer told me that I should tell the Customs Officer that I was in fear for my life due to the drugs and violence that was going on in my country and that I sought asylum in Canada. I told him that wasn't true. I was from the Yucatan and we weren't having any problems with drugs or violence. That was all taking place along the border between Mexico and the United States. He said that I should tell them that threats had been made against my life and that if I returned to Mexico I was going to be killed by the drug lords. I told him that wasn't true, either.

He said that if I wanted to get into Canada that was what I was going to have to say. He explained that once I was in Canada by the time the hearing took place on whether or not I was entitled to be granted asylum in Canada my vacation would be up and I could either go home or else we could try to find some other reason why I should be allowed to stay.

I couldn't do what he suggested. I couldn't bring myself to lie about that. Maybe I should have. It was true that there was much violence in cities like Juarez in the north of Mexico, but that had nothing to do with me. Wars between the drug lords, the Police, the Federales, the Army and with each other are killing thousands of us every year, but not me or my family.

Four hours later, I was put on a plane and sent back to Mexico. I never even saw Rayna. On the airplane ride home, I cried.

As soon as I got back to Mexico I called Rayna and she told me that I should go to the Canadian Consulate and obtain a work visa. She sent me a copy of the letter from the man who had agreed to employ me. I took the letter to the Canadian Embassy and asked for a visa, since that was now required, as I had found out. They told me that before they would let me in the country to work the prospective employer would first have to offer the job to Canadian citizens. If no Canadian citizens took the job, then they would let me in. I applied for a visa, hoping that no Canadians would accept the job.

OFFICE OF CANADIAN CONSULATE
MERIDA, MEXICO

Application Kit for a Temporary Resident Visa
Requirements for a Canadian Temporary Resident Visa.
The documents you provide must satisfy the officer that you meet the requirements of the Immigration and Refugee Protection Act and Regulations. Some of these requirements include satisfying the officer your stay in Canada will be for a temporary period and that:

1. you will leave Canada at the end of your authorized stay;
2. You have enough money to support yourself and your and your family members in Canada and to return home;
3. You do not intend to work or study in Canada unless authorized to do so
4. You are a law abiding and have no record of criminal activity (you may be asked to provide a Police Clearance Certificate;
5. You will not be a risk to the security of Canada; and
6. You have produced any additional documents requested by the officer to establish your admissibility and you are in good health and will complete a medical examination (if required).

A single entry Visa allows you to enter Canada only once. If you intend to travel to the United States during your visit to Canada, you DO NOT need a multiple entry visa in order to re-enter Canada directly from the United States during the period for which you were originally admitted to Canada.

Before August of 2009 Mexicans could enter Canada without a Visa. They could get in with a Passport only. The citizens of Mexico now need Visas to travel to Canada. This requirement applies to all persons who wish to visit the country for business, school, work or other such reasons and all must obtain a temporary visa to Canada. To facilitate your trip, consult www.canada.org.

The problem was that there were plenty of Canadian citizens who would take the job, but they would always quit after a short time. I don't remember what kind of job it was, but I know it wasn't a high-paying desk job. It was the kind of job that only Mexican laborers, or laborers from some other country, like China, Russia, Honduras, Guatemala, El Salvador and other places outside of the United States or Canada would take and be happy with.

Canadians were much like people from the United States. There could be 10% unemployment, like there is now in the United States, but very few of those millions of unemployed people were willing to get out in the fields, or in the factories, or in restaurants and do the menial work for a minimum wage. As Rayna explained, the man said he'd given jobs to Canadians in the past and they had always quit within a few weeks. He said it happened all the time, that's why he was willing to give me a job. The Canadian Embassy didn't see it that way and required him to go through this procedure.

Sure enough, a Canadian accepted the job and my application for a visa was denied. At the present time, my application is being reconsidered. Rayna and I still e-mail each other. She can't wait forever and neither can I. Now I am back in Cancun, taking tourists on scuba diving trips around the beautiful island of Cozumel, which is a paradise.

As I pondered my plight, I realized that I had made many mistakes. There were so many ways I could have legally stayed in the country and become a United States citizen. I had the opportunity to marry American women who would have, in so doing, assisted me in becoming a citizen, but I wanted to marry for love, and love didn't provide me with that opportunity. I could have applied for citizenship as a relative of a citizen in need of assistance, which I could have done when Uncle Otto was ill and Aunt Elba needed assistance. I could have gone through the formal immigration process, but that is a long, tedious process, taking many years with no guarantee of success.

Although less than 100,000 Mexicans are granted Green Cards every year, I am told, I could have entered under a guest worker program. I could have become an H-5A worker. I could have claimed that I was a member of the skilled or professional class, which wasn't too far from the truth, though I possessed no graduate degrees or any extraordinary technical skills. But the best chance I had of staying in the United States and possibly becoming a citizen came by way of an amnesty program, which has been much discussed and debated but yet to be implemented. Now that I am no longer in the United States I am ineligible for amnesty.

Mexico is said to be the 11th largest country in the world, with a population of almost 110 million people, yet 10% of that number are said to be living illegally in the United States at this time. I am no longer one of those 11 million people.

If I am to go with the wind, it will be to another country other than the U.S., unless I go illegally, which I think about doing all the time, but I fear that I will be put in jail and I know better than to try that.

I ask myself why I still want to go back to the United States, a country that does not want me back, especially since my roots are so strong and so deep in the Yucatan, in Mexico and in Progreso in particular. Most people think it is for the money, and it is undoubtedly true that most Mexicans go to the United States to work because of the money, but that is not the case for me. I have worked many different types of jobs, and done them all well, but I have made as much money in Cancun, Playa del Carmen and Isla de Mujeres as I have in the United States, if not more, so money is not the reason for me.

No, it is more than that. It is the people and their attitudes. I love the diversity, too. I like the atmosphere and the feelings I have when in the United States. Everything is new and different for me and there is a feeling of optimism and change. Things need to change in Mexico, and maybe money is all that is needed to bring about that change, plus the elimination of corruption and, most importantly right now, elimination of the drug cartels that are killing so many people, including many innocents, but that will take many years.

Some say amnesty should be granted to all who have stayed out of trouble, paid taxes and worked hard. Others say that all illegals like me should be kicked out of the country and kept out. Other plans are somewhere in between, saying that people who have been in the United States illegally for over five years should be granted amnesty and the rest sent home. President Obama plans to address the issue soon, but I am not sure it will help someone like me. We will see.

I have come to love the United States and its people and it is there that I would like to live, but since I can't do that I am thinking of moving to Spain at the moment, or maybe Argentina, or Brazil, but for whatever reasons, maybe it is the poet in me, or maybe it is simply wanderlust, but I must go. I am a traveler.

A Traveler

I am a traveler. I risk my life in each adventure I take;
I know the fear of losing my life and yet I take the risk;
When I survive a danger, I live again;
I seek to be as consistent as the sun which rises
in the morning and sets at night;
To be at peace with the immense universe, able to hear
the music of the cosmos in moments of silence;
I am like one of the smallest of stars in the
heavenly skies, I am a part of all that is;
I follow the wind; I note all that I see; I am a poet;

APPENDIX

Author's Note: The following was the law in the United States in 2005 when Jorge was arrested. It is a document given Jorge by the American Immigration Lawyers Association and it represents their summary and analysis of the 2005 Secure America and Orderly Immigration Act. They have allowed me to reprint it in its entirety.

At the time of writing, President Obama has pledged to address the problem with our immigration system and to overhaul it dramatically, which may include amnesty or some form thereof, stricter guidelines, more severe penalties, more open borders, more secure borders or some combination thereof. However, as of January, 2011, there the law as found below remains the law of our land. Though I am a lawyer, I had never read this prior to writing this book. It is my thought that many readers would like to know what the law regarding immigration is and so I include it herein.

The Secure America and Orderly Immigration Act of 2005

Section 1. Short Title and Table of Contents

The Act may be cited as the Secure America and Orderly Immigration Act.

Section 2 Findings

This section makes a number of congressional findings on, among other things, the need to secure our borders; the contributions of immigrants and the need for our immigration policies to reflect our tradition as a nation of immigrants; the need for a comprehensive approach to solving our immigration problems, the provision of adequate channels for legal immigration and strong enforcement of laws that serve our economic, social and security interests.

TITLE I: BORDER SECURITY

Section 101: Definitions

This section defines the following terms: "appropriate congressional committees,: "international border of the United States," "Secretary" and "security plan."

Subtitle A: Border Security Strategic Planning

Section 111: National Strategy for Border Security

Section 111 directs the Secretary of Homeland Security (Secretary) to develop and implement a National Strategy for Border Security (Strategy) to protect the international borders of the United States. The Strategy must include: (1) identification and evaluation of points of entry and portions of the border that must be protected from illegal transit; (2) a design for the most appropriate and cost-effective means of defending the border against threats, including advancements in technology, equipment, personnel, and training needed to address security vulnerabilities; (3) risk-based priorities for assuring border security including deadlines for addressing security and enforcement needs; (4) coordination among federal, state, regional, local and tribal authorities to provide for effective border management and security enforcement; (5) a prioritization of research and development objectives to enhance border security and enforcement needs; (6) an update of the 2001 Port of Entry Infrastructure Assessment Study that was conducted by the legacy U.S. Customs Service and General Services Administration; (7) strategic interior enforcement coordination plans with personnel of Immigration and Customs Enforcement; (8) strategic enforcement coordination plans with overseas personnel of the Department of Homeland Security and State to end human smuggling and trafficking activities; (9) any other appropriate infrastructure, security plans or reports the Secretary deems appropriate for inclusion; (10) the identification of low-risk travelers and how such identification would facilitate cross-border travel; and (11) ways to ensure that U.S.

trade and commerce are not diminished by efforts, activities, and programs aimed at securing the homeland.

The Strategy shall be the governing document for federal security and enforcement efforts related to securing the borders.

Section 112: Reports to Congress

Within one year of enactment, the Secretary must submit the National Strategy for Border Security to the appropriate congressional committees. Subsequent revisions of the Strategy must be submitted every two years. Each year, in conjunction with the submission of the budget to Congress, the Secretary must submit a progress report on the implementation of the Strategy and each security plan, as well as any recommendations for improvement.

Section 113: Authorization of Appropriations

This section authorizes the appropriations necessary to carry out the provisions of this subtitle for each of the 5 fiscal years beginning with the fiscal year following the year of enactment.

Subtitle B: Border Infrastructure, Technology Integration and Security Enhancement.

Section 121 requires the Secretary to coordinate, develop and implement a plan with federal, state, local and tribal authorities on law enforcement, emergency response, and security-related responsibilities with regard to the international border. The plan should ensure that the security of the border is not compromised: (1) when the jurisdiction for providing security changes from one authority to another; (2) in areas where jurisdiction is shared among authorities; or (3) when one authority relinquishes jurisdiction to another authority pursuant to a memorandum of understanding. In developing the plan, the Secretary must consider methods to coordinate emergency responses, improve data sharing, communications, and technology, and promote research and development relating to the aforementioned. Within one year of implementing the plan described above, the Secretary must submit a report on its development and implementation to the appropriate congressional committees.

Section 122: Border Security Advisory Committee

Section 122 authorizes the Secretary to establish and appoint a Border Security Advisory Committee to provide advice and recommendations to the Secretary on border security and enforcement issues. The advisory Committee must be comprised of members who represent a broad cross-section of perspectives, including representatives from border states, local law enforcement agencies, community officials, and tribal authorities of border states, and other interested parties.

Section 123: Programs on the Use of Technologies for Border Security

Section 123 requires the Secretary, within 60 days of enactment, to develop and implement a program to enhance border security through the utilization of aerial surveillance technologies. The Secretary must consider current and proposed aerial surveillance technologies, assess the feasibility of utilizing such technologies which the Secretary may deploy along the border, and consult with the Administrator of the FAA regarding safety and airspace coordination and regulation.

The program shall utilize a variety of aerial surveillance technologies in a variety of topographies and areas for a range of circumstances, as well as unmanned aerial vehicles. Within one year of implementing the program, the Secretary must submit to the appropriate congressional committees a report that includes a description of the program and the Secretary's recommendations for enhancing the program.

Section 123 also authorizes the Secretary, as part of the development and implementation of the National Strategy for Border Security, to establish and carry out demonstration programs to strengthen communication, information sharing, technology, security, intelligence benefits, and enforcement activities that will protect the border without diminishing trade and commerce.

Section 124: Combating Human Smuggling

Section 124 requires the Secretary to develop and implement a plan to improve coordination between the Bureau of Immigration and Customs Enforcement, the Bureau of Customs and Border Protection and other federal, state, local and tribal authorities to combat human smuggling. In developing the plan, the Secretary must consider the interoperability of databases used to prevent human smuggling; adequate and effective personnel training; methods and programs to effectively combat human smuggling; the effective utilization of visas for victims of trafficking (T-visas) and other crimes; investigatory techniques, equipment, and procedures that prevent, detect and prosecute international money laundering and other smuggling operations; joint measures with the Secretary of State to enhance intelligence sharing and cooperation with foreign governments; and any other measures that the Secretary considers appropriate. The Secretary must submit a report to Congress on the plan within one year of its implementation, including any recommendations for legislative action to improve efforts to combat human smuggling.

Section 125: Savings Clause

Section 125 provides that nothing in Subtitles A or B of Title I may be construed to provide any state or local entity any additional authority to enforce Federal immigration laws.

SUBTITLE C—International Border Enforcement

Section 131: North American Security Initiative

Section 131 requires the Secretary of State to establish a framework for better management, communication and coordination between the Governments of North America in order to enhance the security and safety of the United States.

Section 132: Information Sharing Agreements

This section authorizes the Secretary of State, in coordination with the Secretary of Homeland Security and the Government of Mexico, to negotiate an agreement with Mexico to cooperate in screening of third-country nationals using Mexico as a corridor to the United States and to provide technical support to enhance immigration control along the Mexican border.

Section 133: Improving the Security of Mexico's Southern Border

Section 133 requires the Secretary of State, in coordination with the

Secretary of Homeland Security, the Canadian Department of Foreign Affairs, and the Government of Mexico, to establish a program to assess the needs of the governments of Central America in maintaining security of their borders. The program will also determine the financial and technical support needed to enhance security and provide technical assistance to the governments of Central America to secure the issuance of passports and travel documents to those countries. In addition, the program will encourage the governments of Central America to control alien smuggling and trafficking, and to prevent the use and manufacturing of fraudulent travel documents. It should also encourage the governments of Central American countries to share relevant information with Mexico, Canada and the United States.

The Secretary of Homeland Security, in coordination with the Secretary of State and the appropriate officials of the governments of Central American countries, must provide robust law enforcement assistance to Central American governments to address migratory issues to enable these governments to dismantle human smuggling organizations and gain tighter control over their borders.

The Secretary of State, in consultation with the Secretary of Homeland Security, the Government of Mexico, appropriate officials of the Governments of Guatemala, Belize, and neighboring contiguous countries, must establish a program to provide needed equipment, technical assistance, and vehicles to manage, regulate and patrol the international border between Mexico and Guatemala and Mexico and Belize.

This section also mandates that the Secretary of State work in coordination with the Secretary of Homeland Security, the Director of the Federal Bureau of Investigation, the Government of Mexico, and the appropriate officials of the governments of Central American countries, to monitor the impact of deporting violent criminal aliens, track Central American gang activities, devise a mechanism for notification of deportation, and share information relevant to gang activities.

Title II: State Criminal Alien Assistance

Section 201: State Criminal Alien Assistance Program Authorization of Appropriations.

Section 201 reauthorizes the State Criminal Alien Assistance Program for Fiscal Years 2005-2011, and provides that such funds may only be made available for correctional purposes.

Section 202: Reimbursement of States for Indirect Costs Relating to the Incarceration of Illegal Aliens.

Section 202 establishes a new program to authorize funding to pay the indirect costs incurred by states for incarcerating illegal aliens. These "indirect costs" include court costs, county attorney costs, detention costs, criminal proceedings expenditures that do not involve going to trial, indigent defense costs, and unsupervised probation costs. Reimbursements must be allocated in a manner that gives special consideration to any State that shares a border with Mexico or Canada or to any State that includes an area in which a large number of undocumented aliens reside relative to the general population. To carry out this section, appropriations are authorized in the amount of $200 million for each of fiscal years 2005-2011.

Section 203: Reimbursement of States for Pre-Conviction Costs Relating to the Incarceration of Illegal Aliens.

Section 203 amends INA section 241(i)(3)(A) to provide for the reimbursement to states for the pre-conviction costs relating to the incarceration of undocumented criminal aliens.

TITLE III: ESSENTIAL WORKER VISA PROGRAM

Section 301: Essential Workers

Section 301 amends INA section 101(a)(15)(H) to create a new essential worker category (to be known as H-5A) for persons coming temporarily to the United States to initially perform labor or services other than those occupation classifications covered under INA 101(a)(15)(H)(i)(b), (H)(ii)(a), (L), (O), (P), or (R). Spouses and children would be eligible to accompany or follow to join the principal alien.

Section 302: Admission of Essential Workers

Section 302 authorizes the Secretary of State to grant a temporary H-5A visa to an alien who demonstrates that he or she is capable of performing the labor or services required for an H-5A occupation and provides the consular officer with evidence of employment in the United States. Such evidence of employment must be provided through the Employment Eligibility Confirmation System established under new INA section 274E, or in accordance with requirements issued by the Secretary of State in consultation with the Secretary of Homeland Security. The non-immigrant worker is required to pass a criminal and security background check, pay a $500 application fee, and undergo a medical examination. Certain grounds of inadmissibility may be waived upon payment of a $1,500 fine.

The H-5A visa shall initially be authorized for three years, and may be extended for one additional three year period. The alien must be employed during the alien's stay in the United States, but may change employers at will. If the alien is unemployed for more than 45 consecutive days, his or her period of authorized admission will terminate and the alien will be required to return to his or her country of nationality or last residence. An alien who returns home due to unemployment may re-enter the United States to work using the same visa, provided the alien meets the same standards required for the initial entry. Aliens holding H-5A visas may travel outside of the United States and be readmitted on the same visa, assuming the period of authorized admission has not expired. The three year period of authorized admission shall not be extended due to the time the alien spends outside the country. Aliens in H-5A status who willfully violate any material term or condition of such status will not be able to renew their status. A waiver is available, however, for technical violations, inadvertent errors, or violations for which the alien was not at fault.

Section 303: Employer Obligations

Section 303 requires employers of H-5A non-immigrants to comply with all federal, state and local laws, including laws affecting migrant and seasonal agricultural workers and the requirements under new INA section 274E, as created by Section 402 of this Act.

Section 304: Protection for Workers

Section 304 provides that H-5A visa non-immigrant aliens shall have the same rights as similarly employed U.S. workers under applicable federal, state and local labor and employment laws. Workers under this program shall not be treated as independent contractors. Employers will be held responsible for all applicable federal, state and local taxes with respect to aliens under the H-5A program. In addition, Section 304 provides that employers must provide the same wages, benefits and working conditions to H-5A workers as are provided to similarly employed U.S. workers. Employers may not hire H-5A aliens as replacement workers during a strike or lockout; H-5A aliens may not be required to waive any rights or protections under this Act; employers who have filed an employment-based immigrant visa petition on behalf of the H-5A worker may not threaten to withdraw such petition in retaliation for the alien's exercise of a right protected by this Act. Section 304 also provides whistleblower protection for H-5A employees.

In addition, Section 304 requires that foreign labor contractors (and employers that engage in foreign labor contracting activity) disclose a variety of information to H-5A workers at the time of their recruitment, including, among other things, the location of employment, a description of the duties, compensation, benefits provided and any associated costs, existence of any labor dispute or labor organizing effort, the extent of any insurance coverage, any education or training required or provided, and a statement describing the protections of this Act. Foreign labor contractors are prohibited from providing false or misleading information and may not assess any fees to the worker for such recruitment. Section 304 requires registration and certification of foreign labor contractors who recruit workers under this program, and further requires the Secretary of Labor to promulgate regulations to establish a process for the investigation and approval of an application for a certificate of registration of foreign labor contractors. Such certificates will be valid for two years, and the Secretary may refuse to issue or renew, or may suspend or revoke a certificate of registration.

This section also provides remedies for foreign labor contractor violations, and requires the Secretary of Labor to prescribe regulations for the receipt, investigation, and disposition of complaints by individuals harmed under this section. In addition, Section 304 sets forth an administrative process under which workers who are harmed by violations of the program can bring a complaint. Remedies and penalties, including both civil and criminal penalties, are also set forth in this section.

Section 105: Market-Based Numerical Limitations

Section 305 provides that 400,000 H-5A visas will be made available for the first fiscal year in which the program is implemented. In any subsequent fiscal year, if the numerical limit is reached within the first quarter, an additional 20% of the allocated number will be made available immediately and the allocated amount for the following fiscal year will increase by 20% of the original allocated amount in the prior fiscal year. If the total number of visas allocated for a given fiscal year is reached in the second quarter of that fiscal year, an additional 15% will be made available immediately and the allocated amount for the following fiscal year will increase by 15% of the original allocated amount in the prior fiscal year. If the total number of visas allocated for a given fiscal year is reached in the third quarter of that fiscal year, an additional 10% will be made available immediately and the allocated amount for the following fiscal year will increase by 10% of the original allocated amount in the prior fiscal year. If the total number of visas allocated for a given fiscal year is reached in the last quarter of that fiscal year, the allocated amount for the following fiscal year will increase by 10% of the original allocated amount in the prior fiscal year. With the exception of the first subsequent fiscal year to fiscal year in which the program is implemented, if the allocated amount is not reached in a given year, and the reason was not due to processing delays or delays in promulgating regulations, the allocated amount will decrease by 10% for the following fiscal year.

Of the total number of visas allocated in a given fiscal year, 50,000 must be allocated to "qualifying counties," defined as counties that are outside a metropolitan statistical area and that, during the 20 year period preceding the date of enactment of this Act, experienced a net out-migration of at least 10%.

Finally, Section 305 provides that, in allocating visas under this section, the Secretary of State may take any additional measures necessary to deter illegal immigration.

Section 306: Adjustment to Lawful Permanent Resident Status

Section 306 amends INA section 245 to provide for adjustment to lawful permanent resident status for eligible aliens admitted under the H-5A program, either through employer based petitions or, if the alien has maintained H-5A status in the U.S. for a cumulative total of four years, through self-petition. Applicants for adjustment under this section must be physically present in the U.S. and establish that they meet the requirements of INA section 312 (setting forth the English language and civics requirements for naturalization applicants) or be satisfactorily pursuing a course of study to achieve such knowledge. Aliens will not be deemed ineligible for H-5A nonimmigrant status solely by virtue of the fact that they have filed for adjustment of status or have otherwise sought permanent residence in the U.S.

Section 306 authorizes the Secretary of Homeland Security to extend the stay of an H-5A nonimmigrant beyond the period of authorized stay if a labor certification or immigrant visa petition filed on behalf of the alien is pending. In such cases, the alien's stay shall be extended in one-year increments until a final decision is made on his or her lawful permanent residence.

Section 307: Essential Worker Visa Program Task Force

Section 307 establishes the Essential Worker Visa Program Task Force to study the Essential Worker Visa Program and make recommendations to Congress. The Task Force will be comprised of 10 persons who will represent a variety of pertinent areas of expertise. The members shall be appointed by the President and leadership of both Houses of Congress and no one party may constitute a majority of the membership. The Task Force must submit a report to Congress within two years of the essential worker program's implementation, the criteria for admission of the temporary worker, the formula for determining the yearly numerical limitation, and the program's impact on immigration, the U.S. workforce and U.S. businesses. A final report must be submitted no later than four years after the submission of the initial report.

Section 308: Willing Worker-Willing Worker Job Registry

Section 308 requires the Secretary of Labor to direct the coordination and modification of the national system of public labor exchange services (known as America's Job Bank) to incorporate essential worker employment opportunities available to United States workers and nonimmigrant workers. Employers seeking to hire H-5A non-immigrants must attest that they have posted the employment opportunity in the Job registry for at least 30 days in an attempt to recruit U.S. workers. Employers must maintain a record of such recruitment efforts for one year and must demonstrate why U.S. workers who applied were not hired.

The Secretary of Labor must ensure that job opportunities advertised on the electronic job registry are accessible by state workforce agencies and that the Internet-based job registry may be accessed by workers, employers, labor organizations and other interested parties.

Section 309: Authorization of Appropriations

Section 309 authorizes appropriations as necessary to carry out this title for each fiscal year beginning with the date of enactment through the sixth fiscal year beginning after implementation of this title.

TITLE IV. ENFORCEMENT

Section 401: Document and Visa Requirements

Section 401 provides that, no later than six months from the date of enactment of this Act, all new visas issued by the Secretary of State and immigration-related documents issued by the Secretary of Homeland Security must be machine-readable and tamper-resistant, use biometric identifiers, and be compatible with the United States Visitor and Immigrant Status Indicator Technology and the employment verification system established under INA section 274E, as added by Section 402 below. The information contained on the visas or immigration-related documents must include: the alien's name, date and place of birth; alien registration or visa number and, if applicable, social security number; the alien's citizenship and immigration status in the U.S.; and the date that the alien's authorization to work in the U.S. expires, if appropriate.

Section 402: Employment Eligibility Confirmation System

Section 402 adds a new section 274E to the INA, requiring the Commissioner of Social Security, in coordination with the Secretary of Homeland Security, to establish an Employment Eligibility Confirmation System to allow **employers to verify an employee's identity and employment authorization. The new system, which will gradually replace the existing I-9 system, will use machine-readable documents that contain encrypted electronic information to verify employment eligibility within <u>one</u> working day after the initial inquiry.** Section 402 also requires the establishment of a secondary verification process to be used in cases of a tentative nonconfirmation. In such cases, the employer **must make the secondary verification inquiry within 10 days of receiving the tentative nonconfirmation.** If an employee chooses to contest a secondary nonconfirmation, the employer must provide the employee with a referral letter and instruct the employee to visit an office of the DHS or the SSA to resolve the discrepancy within 10 working days of receipt of the referral letter. An individual's failure to contest a confirmation will not constitute knowledge, as that term is defined in 8 CFR section 274a.1(1).

As a safeguard against erroneous information, individuals will be able to view their records in the system. The Commissioner of Social Security, in coordination with the Secretary of Homeland Security, will provide a process by which individuals may correct false information. This section also sets forth various unlawful uses of the system that shall be considered unlawful immigration-related employment practices.

Employers are required to notify employees and prospective employees of the use of the Employment Eligibility Confirmation System and that the system may be used for enforcement purposes. In addition, employers must verify the identity and employment authorization status of new H-5A employees within three days of hire and must provide a copy of the employment verification receipt to such employees. Section 402 provides for an affirmative defense against violations based upon good faith compliance with the requirements of this section. This section requires the Commissioner of Social Security, in coordination with the Secretary of Homeland Security, to the extent practicable, to implement an interim system to confirm employment eligibility before implementation of the new Employment Eligibility Confirmation System.

In addition, Section 402 requires the Commissioner of Social Security, in coordination with the Secretary of Homeland Security and other appropriate agencies, to design, implement, and maintain an Employment Eligibility Database, which will be implemented gradually, and will include employment eligibility data for **all individuals who are not citizens or nationals of the U.S. but who are authorized or seeking authorization to be employed in the U.S.** The Commissioner of Social Security is required to establish a system to annually reverify the employment eligibility of each individual described in this section. Access to the new database will be limited and provisions to protect against the unauthorized disclosure of the information contained in the database must be established.

Finally, Section 402 requires the Comptroller General of the United States to submit to the House and Senate Judiciary Committee, no later than 3 months after the last day of the second and third years that the system is in effect, a report on the new Employment Eligibility Confirmation System, including: an assessment of the impact of the system on the employment of unauthorized workers; an assessment of the accuracy of the Employment Eligibility Database and Social Security Administration databases and the timeliness and accuracy of responses to employers; an assessment of the privacy, confidentiality and system security of the system; an assessment of whether the system is being implemented in a nondiscriminatory manner; and any recommendations on whether the system should be modified.

Section 403: Improved Entry and Exit Data System

This section amends section 110 of the Illegal Immigration Reform and Immigrant Responsibility Act of 1996 to make various technical corrections and provide for the collection of **biometric machine-readable information from an alien's visa or immigration-related documents upon arrival and departure from the U.S. to determine the alien's status.**

Section 404: Department of Labor Investigative Authorities

This section provides the Secretary of Labor with the authority to initiate **investigation of employers employing H-5A non immigrants if the Secretary of her designee certifies that reasonable cause exists to believe that the employer is out of compliance** with the Secure America and Orderly Immigration Act or INA section 274E. This section also sets forth various criteria for determining whether such reasonable cause exists.

Section 405: Protection of Employment Rights

Section 405B directs the Secretaries of Labor and Homeland Security to establish a process by which H-2B and H-5A nonimmigrants, who file non-frivolous complaints regarding an employer's violation under the program, may seek other appropriate employment under their visa.

Section 406: Increased Fines for Prohibited Behavior

This section doubles the existing fines for unfair employment practices under INA sections 274B(g)(2)(B)(iv).

TITLE V. PROMOTING CIRCULAR MIGRATION PATTERNS.

Section 501: Labor Migration Facilitation Programs

Section 501 authorizes the Secretary of State to enter into agreements with foreign governments whose citizens participate in the new temporary worker program in an effort to establish and administer joint labor migration facilitation programs. The Secretary of Homeland Security and the Secretary of Labor are also authorized to participate in such programs. The programs would be designed to monitor the foreign workers' participation in the temporary worker program and my address: the facilitation and monitoring of travel between the country of origin and the U.S.; reintegration in the worker's country of origin upon permanent return from the U.S; and any appropriate features to promote the worker's strong ties to his/her country of origin. The Secretary of State must place priority on developing programs with foreign governments that have a large number of nationals working as temporary workers and must enter into such agreements not later than 3 months after the date of enactment or as soon thereafter as is practicable.

Section 502: Bilateral Efforts with Mexico to Reduce Migration Pressures and Costs.

This section contains a series of "findings" and a Sense of Congress Acknowledges the need to assist the Government of Mexico in strengthening Its governance and promoting opportunities for its citizens that will help reduce migration incentives. It also includes a Sense of Congress urging the Governments of the United States and Mexico to enter into a partnership to examine uncompensated and burdensome health care costs incurred by the United States due to legal and illegal immigration by: 1) increasing health care access for poor and underserved populations in Mexico; 2) assisting Mexico in increasing its emergency trauma healthcare facilities along the border; 3) facilitating the return of stable, incapacitated workers to Mexico to receive long- term care in their home country; and 4) helping the Mexican government to establish a program with the private sector to cover the health care needs of its citizens working in the United States.

TITLE VI.: FAMILY UNITY AND BACKLOG REDUCTION

Section 601: Elimination of Existing Backlogs

This section exempts immediate relatives (spouses, children, and parents of U.S. citizens) from the annual level of 480,000 for family-sponsored immigrant visas. Unused family-sponsored immigrant visas from previous fiscal years are recaptured and made available for family-sponsored immigrant visas for future fiscal years. The level of employment based immigrant visas is increased from 140,000 to 290,000 per fiscal year. Unused employment-based immigrant visas from previous fiscal years are recaptured and made available for employment-based immigrant visas for future fiscal years.

Section 602: Country Limits

Section 602 increases the per country limits for family-sponsored and employment-based immigrants from 7% to 10% (in the case of countries) and from 2% to 5% (in the case of dependent areas).

Section 603: Allocation of Immigrant Visas

Section 603 redistributes the 480,000 family-sponsored immigrant numbers among existing family preference categories, as follows:

10% is allocated to the first preference-unmarried sons and daughters of U.S. citizens. 50% is allocated to the second preference-spouses and unmarried sons and daughters of lawful permanent residents, of which 77& of such visas will be allocated to spouses and children of lawful permanent residents. 10% is allocated to the third preference-married sons and daughters of U.S. citizens. 30% is allocated to the fourth preference-brothers and sisters of U.S. citizens.

The 290,000 ceiling for employment-based immigrant visas is redistributed among the employment-based immigrant visa categories and certain modifications are made to current categories. 20% is allocated to the first preference-aliens with **extraordinary ability, outstanding professors and researchers, and multinational executives and managers.** 20% is allocated to the second preference-aliens holding **advanced degrees or having exceptional ability.** 35% is allocated to the third preference-**skilled workers and professionals**. 5% is allocated to a re-designated fourth preference-**investors.** 30% is allocated to a re-designated fifth preference-other **workers performing unskilled labor that is not of a temporary or seasonal nature** (previously included in third preference). Each year, all unused immigrant visas from the first four preference categories will be made available for fifth preference workers.

The current fourth preference category is stricken, so that special immigrants are no longer counted against the employment-based ceiling. Similarly, Section 203 strikes INA section 203(b)(6), which provides special numerical rules for K special immigrants.

Section 604: Relief for Children and Widows

Section 604 extends eligibility for the immediate relative category to the accompanying or following to join children of the children, spouses and parents of U.S. citizens.

In addition, Section 604 provides that surviving spouses, children, and parents who applied for adjustment of status prior to the death of a qualifying relative may have such application adjudicated as if the death had not occurred. Aliens whose qualifying relative died before the enactment and who received a denial of an application for adjustment of status not more than two years before the date of enactment may renew their adjustment application through a motion to reopen, without fee, filed no later than one year after the date of enactment.

Section 605: Amending the Affidavit of Support Requirements

This section lowers the income level required for an affidavit of support from 125% to 100% of the **federal poverty guidelines**.

Section 606: Discretionary Authority

Section 606 grants the Secretary of Homeland Security the discretionary authority to waive certain misrepresentation grounds of inadmissibility for spouses, parents, or sons or daughters of U.S. citizens or lawful permanent residents if the Secretary determines that the refusal of the alien's admission would result in extreme hardship to the U.S. citizen or lawful permanent residence relative. The DHS Secretary may also exercise such discretionary authority in the case of an alien granted classification under clause (iii) or (iv) of INA section 204(a)(I)(A), or clause (ii) of (iii) of section 204 (a)(I)(B), if the alien demonstrates extreme hardship to the alien, or to his or her U.S. citizen, lawful permanent resident, or qualified alien parent or child. Aliens granted such waivers must pay a $2,000 fine.

Section 607: Family Unity

This section raises the maximum age of eligibility for exemption from the 3-10 year bars from 18-21 years of age. In addition, the DHS Secretary is granted discretionary authority to waive the 3-10 year and permanent bars for aliens who, on or before the date of introduction of this Act, had pending family-sponsored or employment-based petitions. Aliens granted such waivers must pay a $2,000 fine.

TITLE VII: H-5B NONIMMIGRANTS

Section 701 adds a new INA section 250A to provide for the adjustment to H-5B nonimmigrant status for an alien who can establish that **he or she was present in the U.S. without authorization <u>before</u> the date of this Act's introduction; and (2) was employed in the U.S. before the date of this Act's introduction, whether full time, part time, seasonally, or self-employed, and has been employed in the U.S. since that date.** The alien's spouse and children are also eligible to apply for adjustment of status or to follow to join the alien. An alien may conclusively establish such employment by submission of employment records maintained by the Social Security Administration, Internal Revenue Service, or by any other federal, state or local government agency; an employer, or a labor union, day labor center, or an organization that assists workers in matters related to employment. Aliens who are unable to submit a document described above may satisfy the requirement of establishing previous employment by submitting at least two of the following types of documents that provide evidence of employment: bank records, business records, sworn affidavits from non-relatives who have direct knowledge of the alien's employment or remittance records. The employment requirements under this section will not apply to minors under 21 years of age. In addition, an alien may satisfy the employment requirements, in whole or in part, by full-time attendance at either an institution of higher education or a secondary school.

An applicant for H-5B status must pay an initial fine of $1,000 in addition to an application fee, submit fingerprints and other data, and undergo criminal and security background checks. An applicant is inadmissible as an H-5B nonimmigrant for grounds related to criminal conduct, security reasons, terrorist activity, or participating in the persecution of any person. Practicing polygamists and child abductors are also barred. However, other grounds of inadmissibility related to undocumented status **will be waived for conduct that occurred before the date of this Act's introduction.**

The period of authorized stay for an H-5B nonimmigrant is **six years,** during which time the Secretary of Homeland Security may not authorize a change from H-5B classification to any other nonimmigrant or immigrant classification. An extension of such status may be granted only to accommodate the processing of an application for adjustment of status under INA section 245B, as added by this section.

An alien who files an application for H-5B status (as well as the alien's spouse or child) will be granted employment authorization, permission to travel abroad, and may not be detained, determined inadmissible or deportable, removed pending final adjudication of the alien's application for adjustment to H-5B status, unless the alien becomes ineligible for such status based upon conduct or criminal conviction. If an alien is apprehended after the date of enactment of this section but before the promulgation of regulations, and the alien can establish prima facie eligibility as an H-5B nonimmigrant, the Secretary of Homeland Security must provide the alien with an opportunity, after promulgation of regulations, to file an adjustment application. In addition, aliens in removal proceedings must be provided the opportunity to apply for adjustment to H-5B status unless a final administrative determination has been made. **Aliens present in the U.S. who have been ordered excluded, deported, removed, or ordered to depart voluntarily** may **not withstanding such order, apply for adjustment to H-5B status. Such aliens will not be required to file motions to reopen, reconsider or vacate.** If the Secretary of Homeland Security grants the application, he must cancel the order. If the application is denied, the original order will be enforceable.

Section 701 also requires the Secretary of Homeland Security to establish an appellate authority within USCIS to provide for a single level of administrative appellate review with respect to applications for adjustment to H-5B status and also provides for judicial review in the federal courts.

This section also provides for the confidentiality of information furnished by H-5B applicants and provides for criminal penalties for violations of the confidentiality provisions. Criminal penalties are also established for false statements made in connection with an H-5B application.

Section 702: Adjustment of Status for H-5B Nonimmigrants

Section 702 adds a new INA section 245B to provide for the adjustment to lawful permanent resident status of an H-5B alien if he or she satisfies the following requirements: (1 completes the employment requirement; (2) pays an additional $1,000 fine as well as the application fee; (3) is admissible under immigration laws; (4) undergoes a medical examination; (5) shows proof of payment of taxes; (6) demonstrates the requisite knowledge of English and U.S. civics; (7) successfully undergoes criminal and security background checks; and (8) registers for military selective service, if applicable. The children and spouse of such an alien may also apply for adjustment.

Section 703: Aliens Not Subject to Direct Numerical Limitations

Section 704: Employer Protections

Section 704 provides that employers of aliens who apply for adjustment of status under this section (either initially, to H-5B status, or from H-5B to permanent resident status) shall not be subject to civil or criminal tax liability relating to the employment of the alien prior to his or her receiving employment authorization.

Section 705: Authorization of Appropriations

This section authorizes funds to the Secretary of Homeland Security to carry out the provisions in this title, and contains a Sense of Congress that such funds should be directly appropriated.

TITLE VIII: PROTECTION AGAINST IMMIGRATION FRAUD

Section 801: Right to Qualified Representation

Section 801 amends INA § 292 to set forth the classes of individuals considered to be authorized representatives for purposes of representation in an immigration matter. This section further provides that only attorneys or individuals approved as accredited representatives under the provisions of this Act may advertise their services to provide representation in an immigration matter. Section 801 also establishes a process by which the Board of Immigration Appeals (BIA) may determine that a person is a "recognized organization" for purposes of designating accredited representatives of the organization to appear in immigration matters. The BIA must approve any qualified individual of a recognized organization as an accredited representative. Such accredited representatives must certify their continuing eligibility for accreditation every 3 years, or will lose their authority to provide representation in immigration matters on behalf of the recognized organization.

Section 801 provides for the right to representation at no cost to the government of individuals in removal proceedings and individuals filing benefits applications, adding that representation by a person other than an authorized representative as described under this section may cause the representative to be subject to civil or other applicable penalties in the case of removal proceedings, and civil or criminal penalties in the case of benefits filings.

Section 801 also proscribes certain representation-related conduct by individuals other than authorized representatives, and provides for civil causes of action for violations thereof. Potential remedies include damages, injunctive relief, attorney's fees, and civil penalties.

Section 802: Protection of Witness Testimony

Section 802 broadens eligibility for a "U" nonimmigrant visa to certain aliens who are determined to be victims of immigration fraud by an unauthorized representative, and raises the numerical limitation on U visas from 10,000 to 15,000 per year.

TITLE IX: CIVICS INTEGRATION

Section 901: Funding for the Office of Citizenship

Section 901 authorizes the Secretary of Homeland Security to establish the United States Citizenship Foundation under the auspices of USCIS. The Foundation is allowed to solicit, accept and make charitable gifts to support the functions of USCIS's Office of Citizenship. This section also authorizes the appropriations necessary to carry out the mission of the Office of Citizenship.

Section 902 directs the Secretary of Homeland Security to establish a competitive grant program to fund entities certified by the Office of Citizenship to provide civics and English classes. The Secretary may accept and use gifts from the United States Citizenship Foundation for grants under this section. Appropriations are authorized as necessary.

TITLE X: PROMOTING ACCESS TO HEALTH CARE

Section 1001: Federal Reimbursement of Emergency Health Services Furnished to Undocumented Aliens

This section extends the authorization for reimbursement of hospitals for the emergency care of undocumented immigrants established under Section 1011 of the Medicare Prescription Drug, Improvement and Modernization Act of 2003 from fiscal years 2008 to 2011 and adds H-5A and H-5B workers to the classes of patients for whom hospitals may be reimbursed.

Section 1002: Prohibition Against Offset of Certain Medicare and Medicaid Payments

Section 1002 provides that payments made under section 1011 of the Medicare Prescription Drug, Improvement and Modernization Act of 2003 shall not be considered "third party coverage" for the purposes of section 1923 of the Social Security Act and shall not impact payments made under such section.

Section 1003: Prohibition Against Discrimination Against Aliens on the Basis of Employment in Hospital-Based Versus Non-Hospital-Based Sites

Section 1003 prohibits state or federal agencies, in determining which aliens will be eligible for waivers of the two-year foreign residence requirement under INA § 212(e) on behalf of an alien described in clause (iii) of such section, from discriminating on the basis of the J visa holder's employment in a hospital-based versus non-hospital-based facility.

Section 1004: Binational Public Health Infrastructure and Health Insurance

Section 1004 requires the Secretary of Health and Human Services to contract with the Institute of Medicine of the National Academies to study binational public health infrastructure and health insurance efforts. Within one year of entering into such contract, the Institute must submit a report to the appropriate congressional committees detailing its recommendations on ways to expand or improve binational public health infrastructure and health insurance efforts.

TITLE XI: MISCELLANEOUS

Section 1101: Submission to Congress of Information Regarding H-5A Nonimmigrants

Section 1101 requires the Secretaries of State and Homeland Security to provide quarterly reports to the House and Senate Judiciary Committees on the number of aliens issued H-5A

nonimmigrant visas or otherwise provided H-5A status during the preceding 3-month period. In addition, the Secretaries must issue more detailed reports to these committees on an annual basis, including statistics on the countries of origin, occupations of, geographic area of employment, and compensation paid to these H-5A workers.

Section 1102: h-5A Nonimmigrant Petitioner Account

This section provides that all petition fees paid by H-5A workers and fees and fines paid by H-5B workers shall be deposited with the U.S. Treasury into the "H-5 Nonimmigrant Petitioner Account." The money in the account will be divided as follows: (a) 53% for the Department of Homeland Security for the adjudication and implementation of the H-5 visa programs and any other efforts necessary to carry out the provisions of this Act. Of that sum, 10% will be directed toward the border security efforts described in Title I of the bill, up to 1% will be used to promote public awareness of the H-5 visa program, to protect migrants from fraud, and to combat the unauthorized practice of law; another 1% will be set aside for the promotion of civics integration activities, and 2% will go to the Civics Integration Grant Program; (b) 15% for Department of Labor enforcement activities; (c) 15% for the Commissioner of Social Security for the creation and maintenance of the Employment Eligibility Confirmation System described in section 402 of the Act; (d) 15% for the Department of State to carry out any necessary provisions of the Act; and (e) 2% for the reimbursement of hospitals serving individuals working under the H-5 programs.

Section 1103: Anti-discrimination

Section 1103 amends INA § 274(a)(3)(B) to include H-5A and H-5B workers in the class of individuals protected under the INA's anti-discrimination provisions.

Section 1104: Women and Children at Risk of Harm

Section 1104 amends INA § 101(a)(27) to render eligible for special immigrant status certain women and children at risk of harm and provides an expedited adjudication process for potential beneficiaries under this section. To be admitted under this section, aliens must pass a background check and must submit fingerprints upon entry. Section 1104 also requires the Secretary of Homeland Security, within one year of enactment, to report to the House and Senate Judiciary Committees on the implementation of this section, including the number of placements.

Section 1105: Expansion of S Visa

Section 1105 expands eligibility for S nonimmigrant status to aliens who are determined to possess critical reliable information concerning the activities of governments or organizations with respect to the development, sale or transfer of weapons of mass destruction and related delivery systems, and who are willing to supply or have supplied such information to the U.S. government. This section also increases the number of aliens who may be granted an S nonimmigrant visa in any given fiscal year from 250 to 3,500.

Section 1106: Volunteers

Section 1106 amends INA § 274(a)(1) to exempt certain religious denominations or organizations from criminal liability for harboring undocumented immigrants if such persons are volunteers with the denominations or organizations, helping them to carry out their vocation.

Appendix B: U. S. Lawful Permanent Residents and Green Cards

(synopsis provided by author)

A lawful permanent resident (LPR) is an individual who has been granted the privilege of residing in the United States on a permanent basis. That person is an immigrant to this country and his status as such remains just that, an immigrant, even though that person is a lawful permanent resident. An LPR can lose permanent resident status if he or she commits an "aggravated felony," which includes smuggling other aliens into the country (other than your spouse, child or parent); money laundering more than $10,000; murder; rape or sexual abuse of a minor; a crime of violence or theft wherein the sentence imposed is for more than a year of incarceration; owning, controlling, managing or supervising a prostitution business; commercial bribery, counterfeiting, forgery and other such things if the sentence is for more than one year of incarceration; and if the person is convicted of a crime involving moral turpitude, among other things.

After being issued an 1-551 Alien Registration Receipt Card, otherwise known as a Green Card, a Lawful Permanent Resident (LPR) may apply for U.S. citizenship after being an LPR for five years. There are other requirements to be met as well, such as residing in the U.S. for at least half of those five years, be of good moral character, be able to demonstrate knowledge and understanding of the fundamentals and principles of the United States, be able to read, write, speak and understand words in ordinary usage in the English language; and take an oath of allegiance to support the Constitution and obey the laws of the United States; renounce any foreign allegiance and/or foreign title; bear arms for the Armed Forces of the United States or perform services for the government of the United States when required, among other things.

There are a number of exceptions and waivers to the foregoing rules and special consideration is frequently given to applicants, depending upon the circumstances of each individual case. The process of filing for a Green Card can be a lengthy one, sometimes involving several years.

By statute, family-based immigration is limited to 480,000 per year. Employment- based immigration is limited to 140,000 per year. The number of refugees allowed into the country is limited as well. That number changes every year. In 1998, the number was 78,000.

According to the Department of Homeland Security's Office of Immigration Statistics, in the calendar year 2009 a total of 1,130,818 persons became LPRs and obtained Green Cards. 59% of those were already living in the United States when granted LPR status. Nearly two-thirds were granted LPR status based on a family relationship with a U.S. citizen or an LPR. 15% of the new LPRs were from Mexico. China at 6% and the Philippines at 5% were the next two.

Epilogue

Before beginning to write this book I researched three different topics involving Jorge's background. The first issue concerned the undocumented aliens from Mexico who are in the United States; the second issue involved Jorge's Mayan heritage; and the third involved the history of Mexico and its relationship to the United States.

Regarding the first issue, that being the issue of the illegal migration of Mexicans to the United States to find work, those of us who are citizens of the United States read about the problem and think of the suggested solutions such as a 2000 mile long wall, a virtual fence, the National Guard patrolling the entire border, armed "Patriots" defending against intruders, and the prosecution of employers who hire such workers, as well as issues such as the rights of undocumented workers to receive health care, housing and other benefits afforded to citizens and many other such issues and we wonder what should be done.

Recently, the state of Arizona has passed a bill into law which requires all those who are not citizens of the United States to carry proof of their identity with them at all times and face arrest if they fail to do so. Just a month ago President Obama signed into law a bill that calls for the expenditure of millions more dollars to protect the borders. This is a very current topic of discussion in our country at present on talk shows, nightly newscasts, law suits and the court of public opinion. Many states are now in the process of passing similar legislation.

Though this book offers no answers to the problem, it puts a face on one of those 'undocumented, illegal aliens' and I hope it helps you, the reader, to reach your own conclusion as to what those answers should be. The issue of what should be done with the illegal immigration issue is extremely complex. No one will deny that the United States needs to protect its borders, both north and south, as well along the coastlines to the east and the west. There are those in the world who have done us harm and seek to do more harm to us.

Therefore, there can be little doubt, it seems, that even if the Mexicans, Guatemalans, Hondurans and other Hispanics aren't the ones most likely to do us harm, if they can make it into the United States, then others who do intend to do us harm can certainly make their way into our country, too. So, clearly, the moneys spent to keep unwanted people out, whether it be by creating fences or walls, are well-spent dollars if they do the job.

Mexicans and others from South and Central America are a virtually unlimited supply of labor that is not only much less expensive than paying American citizens to do the job, but they are also easily manipulated, especially if they are illegal or undocumented laborers. Those who are documented come like commodities...purchased, pursuant to contracts, for prescribed periods of time, usually, and with very specific conditions regarding the terms of their admission to this country and the basis on which they can be here.

Over the last century there have been many such "guest worker" programs. By far the largest and most successful initiative was the Bracero Program which ran from 1942 to 1964. It officially sanctioned and permitted Mexican laborers to come to the United States. They were welcomed with open arms. Their strong arms and backs were needed by a country at war as well as after the war for many years since so many Americans lost their lives during that war.

In 1965, a new program emerged, for a variety of reasons. It was known as the Border Industrialization Program, or BIP. It resulted in the creation of maquiladores, which were and still are foreign-owned assembly plants situated in free trade zones along Mexico's northern border. U.S. manufacturers were invited to move their factories south across the 2000 mile long border to take advantage of much lower wage rates, Mexican subsidies encouraged the rapid growth of industrial parks and regulations allowed manufacturers to import duty-free parts and raw materials.

The BIP program was intended as a way to allow Mexico to absorb back into its country the workers who had been part of the Bracero, or guest worker program, but it has proven to be quite lucrative for the manufacturers since they get the benefits of cheap labor, cheap parts needed in production, plus subsidies and a free trade, or no tax, zone. As a result of that program there are at least fourteen large population centers, such as Tijuana-San Diego, Ciudad Juarez-El Paso, Nuevo Laredo-Laredo and so forth, where some 12 million Mexicans work. Mexican workers are paid a fraction of what U.S. citizens would make, and there are no unions or organized labor pools who are represented by knowledgeable lawyers or negotiators.

In 2005, over $100 billion worth of goods were produced by the 4000 maquiladoras, which employed over one and a half million Mexicans. This, of course, is a small fraction of what Mexican laborers do for the U.S. economy. Most of those jobs were in factories, on assembly lines, not out in the fields of agriculture, where over ten times that many Mexicans work, not to mention workers from Honduras, Nicaragua, El Salvador and other countries across Central and South America.

NAFTA, or the North American Free Trade Agreement, was enacted in 1994 with the expressed purpose of expanding commerce between the U.S., Mexico and Canada. It also provided that Mexico would not interfere with the operations of foreign corporations, favor domestic corporations over foreign corporations or force corporations to share technology with local hosts. Obviously, Mexico did not have nearly as much technology to share with the U.S. or Canada, and it would not be able to reap the knowledge from its northern neighbors.

The worst part of NAFTA for Mexicans was that it opened up Mexico to U.S. corporations which were better able to market their goods to Mexicans than Mexican corporations were able to market their goods to the U.S. or to Canada. Most importantly, corn, the single most important product to the Mexican economy since the days of the Mayans, was now being sold to Mexicans at prices lower than Mexican farmers could compete with, forcing small and subsistence level farmers of corn, who relied on government subsidies to survive, out of business.

NAFTA was America's answer to the European Economic Union and its single currency, the Euro. The two agreements symbolize the growing globalization our world is experiencing. The marketplace is now the entire world, not just a local city, state or country, especially so with the growth of internet sales. The effect of that process was to further expand the need for cheap labor domestically to compete with the ridiculously low labor costs in places like China, Taiwan, Vietnam, Cambodia and other such places in Asia, where many American corporations, which have become multi-national corporations, are now conducting business.

Of course, the issue of what income is taxable in the United States, whether off-shore tax havens can be reached, and if foreign corporations doing business in the United States should have tariffs to level the playing field are entirely different subjects. For Mexicans, NAFTA has meant more problems and less income. There are many Americans who question its usefulness and effectiveness, though it has provided some financial rewards for the U.S.

There are those in Mexico who think that there is an unspoken conspiracy, or a hidden agenda, for the corporations who employ illegal aliens, especially those who knowingly do so. The undocumented aliens, those who are in the country without formal papers allowing them to do so, or those without 'documents,' are less likely to complain to authorities, less likely to organize themselves to negotiate better pay, better living conditions or better working conditions, less likely to seek medical attention or redress from the law for job-related injuries, and less likely to leave a job, because their livelihoods are so hand-to-mouth.

That said, despite the poor pay, poor working conditions, poor living conditions and all the rest, Mexicans still throng to the United States because they are able to earn so much more in the United States than they could in Mexico. Corporations who employ "legal" Mexicans pay much more to them in wages and benefits than they do to the "illegal" Mexicans. Also, less money is paid by those employers to both the United States government and the Mexican government in administrative fees and taxes. It would seem clear that it is in their best interests to employ undocumented aliens.

Bill Clinton, the only Democratic President from 1980 until Barach Obama was elected in 2008, did as much or more than any Republican president to repress immigration from Mexico. His "Operation Gatekeeper" program, and later the Anti-terrorism and Effective Death Act, plus the Illegal Immigration Reform and Immigrant

Responsibility Act represented a "get tough" on immigrants attitude. On his watch things like a wall between the U.S. and Mexico; militias, Minutemen, use of National Guardsmen and soldiers along the border came into existence. A dramatic increase in funding for the U.S. Border Patrol occurred but that amount was magnified ten-fold after 9-11.

It can fairly be asked, other than the criminal element involved in drug-trafficking, and the druglords, what have Mexicans done to threaten the safety of the United States? Is it fair to link the poor Mexican immigrants who risk their lives to come to the United States to work in menial, back-breaking, low-paying jobs and live in squalor while doing so with those who destroyed the World Trade Center and would eliminate the "white-devils" off the face of the earth? I think not, but that is the effect, if not the intent.

There is another aspect of the immigration problem to consider, and that is the issue of incarceration of illegals. Under the Operation Gatekeeper program, people found to be illegally in the country began to receive much longer prison sentences and many more people were incarcerated, prompting the construction of more and more penal facilities, or prisons, to house them. There is much money being made from such a business.

Operation Gatekeeper also provided for sanctions, including stiff fines and other penalties for those who hired illegal immigrants, but the Bush administration, and the Clinton administration before it, failed to enforce that aspect of the problem, though an enormous amount of time, effort, money and resources were expended to find and punish the illegals, many of which were women and children. The employers were not punished nearly as often or as severely.

The policy which the United States has towards its neighbors to the south has changed dramatically over the last hundred and fifty years and it is still changing. Most of the lands west of the Mississippi were under the control of the Aztecs prior to 1500; then it was under the control of the Spanish up until 1821; and then the Mexicans until the Mexican-American war ended when the land became part of the United States. When the truce was signed in 1848 the people who lived there at that time were, technically, Mexicans, disregarding the native American Indians altogether, which is what all countries did. There was no policy in effect at that time and people came and went across the border as they pleased.

Many Americans don't know that when the United States declared war on Mexico in 1846 and attacked Mexico, the treaty that was entered into at the point of guns and cannons put the border along the Rio Grande River in south Texas and extended it to San Diego, and it gave not only Texas to the United States but also California, Arizona, New Mexico, Colorado, Utah, Wyoming and parts of Oregon. Many other concessions were made as a part of that treaty, too, such as the right of Americans to conduct business in the Mexico. Many Americans bought land and established businesses in Mexico, big businesses such as oil and gas exploration, the railroads and other things.

In 1910, the revolution led by Pancho Villa and Zapata declared that all lands in Mexico were owned by Mexicans and it eliminated all rights of foreigners, mostly Americans, to their holdings. Though it is a bit like "whistling Dixie," some Mexicans persist with the argument that Mexico and Mexicans have a right to be in California, Arizona, New Mexico and the other states since those lands were wrongfully taken from them, just as lands were wrongfully taken from the Native American Indians, or just as the Soviet Union under Stalin wrongfully usurped control over many countries which surrounded Russia, or any other examples in history where one country took over another country by military force. It is an unrealistic position to take, but it is a point that some want to include in the debate over whether or not Mexicans should be allowed into the United States.

The history between the two countries dates back to the early to mid-1800s, about the time Texas was being settled. For nearly a century, there was never a problem for Mexicans to enter the United States or vice-versa. Mexican laborers have been employed in the fields and vineyards for over a hundred years now. They came and went without any problems whatsoever during most of those years. It wasn't until 1917 when the United States first took a position to control the flow of people coming into our country from anywhere else in the world. There were a few brief periods of time when papers, or documents, were required, but for most of that time none were. Rather, as Emma Lazarus wrote in 1883, the United States welcomed all who wished to enter. Her words at the beginning of this book are found at the base of the Statue of Liberty.

Since 1986, however, the issue of "undocumented" Mexicans has become a major political issue in the United States. No one can deny that laborers from Mexico are needed to work in the fields, restaurants and factories in America since, although the unemployment rate is currently very high, most Americans are unwilling or unable to do the jobs that Mexicans perform and, someway, somehow over eleven million people are finding jobs in our country, so it seems undeniable that there is a demand for their services.

No one wants to bend over and pick strawberries, or cotton or pick oranges and apples from trees off of ladders for eight or ten back-breaking hours seven days a week, while living in ramshackle housing with inadequate facilities and being underpaid, too. Until there is no need for Mexican labor there will be laborers coming from Mexico to the United States by the millions, as is the case now. The problem is with the documentation, not the demand or the supply. The reasons for the problem can be and are being debated right now in Congress and in homes all across America, and what cannot be decided is how to solve the problem.

President Obama promises to reform immigration laws but no one knows how he will do so. Will he favor an amnesty program? Will he favor a more stringent policy against those who employ illegals? Will he want even tougher laws on protecting the borders? Or will he require better documentation of workers? He sent in an additional one thousand National Guardsmen to the Texas/Arizona/New Mexico border on May 28, 2010. Regardless of what Obama wants, what will Congress agree to? What will the new policy be towards Mexican workers who come to the United States to perform the tasks that no Americans seem to want to do?

There is a 10% unemployment rate in the United States currently yet there are supposedly over eleven million people working illegally in the United States from Mexico alone. How can that be other than that Americans don't want to do the jobs which the illegals are willing to perform? Maybe employers purposefully employ the illegals, as suggested above. Many scoff at the suggestion that the jobs performed by Mexicans are "beneath" what Americans are willing to do when so many Americans desperately need jobs.

However, the numbers are so overwhelming that it simply can't be denied that the United States has a need for workers from Mexico and other places to do the work that American business owners need to have done, regardless of whether or not Americans are willing to perform those jobs. The statistical data over the last seventy years bears that out. Therefore, it seems to me, the only real question to be decided is how to provide for the orderly admission of those Mexican workers, and workers from other countries as well, who are needed in the United States through the use of documentation.

The immigration reform act passed in 2005 has not worked. Everyone seems to agree that another comprehensive immigration reform bill is necessary but it is an extremely sensitive issue which Congress was unwilling to address during the 2010 election year yet the Federal government refuses to allow states, like Arizona, to deal with the problem on their own.

Arizona's new law is said to be the toughest anti-immigration law in the country. It went into effect at the end of July, 2010. The law requires police to ask for immigration papers from anyone whom they have a "reasonable suspicion" might be in the country illegally AFTER the individual is stopped for an otherwise lawful reason. Law enforcement officials are empowered to detain anyone they hold in such suspicion. 25 other states supposedly are in the process of enacting similar laws.

In Arizona, it is a crime for an immigrant to be found without immigration papers, much like a driver must always have a driver's license with him or her. Incredibly, individual citizens can sue the government if the Arizona government, whether it is city, county or state law enforcement officials, fail to enforce the law. Anyone found to be illegally in the state is said to be a trespasser and can be jailed for up to six months and/or fined up to $2500, which is more stringent than the punishment provided by the Federal government, which mainly threatens deportation. It is also a crime for a citizen to provide aid to a known illegal immigrant. A Federal Judge in Phoenix found parts of the new law unconstitutional and her decision is now being appealed.

Since approximately 30% of Arizona is comprised of people with Hispanic ancestry, and it is estimated that far in excess of 80% of the illegal immigrants are Hispanic, it is hard to figure how police won't apprehend many Hispanics, based on their appearance alone, who are lawful residents of Arizona. That is called "racial profiling," much like stopping each and every person of Middle-Eastern ancestry after 9-11 as being a potential terrorist, or people with long hair during the seventies on suspicion of drug usage.

No matter what is done there will undoubtedly still be those who will want to get into the U.S. if they are not among those selected to be workers. There were some problems with the Bracero program, which was also called the 'guest worker' program, but it would seem that there is no other logical choice, other than to open the borders completely and allow workers to move to and from Mexico and Canada, and other countries, conceivably, without limitation, just as is done in Europe with those countries who are part of the European Economic Union. Our politicians have yet to dictate how our immigration policy is to be changed as of the time this book goes to press.

As for Jorge, I'm sure he would do things differently if he had them to do over again, which he doesn't. It would seem as if he would have been an ideal candidate for becoming a legal immigrant to the United States. He could also have obtained a work permit, if time would have allowed him to do so. He could have married an American woman and become a legal resident.

There are and there were other ways for him to have come to the United States and visit, legally, but not work, and stay as long as he wanted to. The 'rub' is, of course, that Jorge couldn't come to the United States without proper papers, work, and stay as long as he wanted to WHENEVER he wanted to. He could do it illegally, and that's what he did. It seems as if Jorge was welcomed in the United States by all who know him but, in the end, unless and until the law is changed, everyone, regardless of race, creed, age, sexual preference, color or national origin must obey the law.

Since Jorge didn't follow the prescribed methods of gaining entry to the U.S., he was subject to the law. He had able counsel representing him and, apparently, despite the many letters in support of Jorge, letters which testified to his good character, his decision to voluntarily depart was his only option, since he would not have been successful had he chosen to fight deportation by way of a trial. In the final analysis, I agree with what Judge Cramer said when he signed the order allowing Jorge to voluntarily depart the country—"Why do I have to deport this man? Why can't you round up the drug dealers and criminals and let me deport them?"

He looked at Jorge and said, "Mr. Frias, I wish there was something I could do to help you, but there isn't. I am bound to follow the follow and the law requires that you leave the country. I will allow you to voluntarily depart and I will give you plenty of time to do so, but you must depart. I wish you good luck."

Regarding the second issue in the book, that being Jorge's Mayan heritage, I found it to be biting irony that Friar de Landa, a Franciscan bishop who was given the authority to Christianize the pagans in the Yucatan immediately after the Yucatan was conquered, destroyed almost all of the Mayan writings, and thousands upon thousands of artifacts, declaring them to be the work of pagans. He destroyed many of the sculptures and works of art as well, declaring them to be idolatry.

It is ironic because most of what is known about the Mayan civilization comes from Friar de Landa. One resource indicated that 95% of what we know of the Mayans comes from de Landa. He was stripped of his control after church leaders learned of what he had done to the Mayan artifacts. He wrote his recollections of what he had learned of the Mayan culture after being stripped of his power. His book is entitled *Yucatan Before and After the Conquest* (Forgotten Books, 1937).

Jorge has studied Mayan culture and visited all of the archeological sites that have been discovered so far, and he is proud of his Mayan heritage. Neither he nor anyone else on the planet knows why the Mayans abandoned their magnificent temples and went back to live in the jungle.

It could have been lack of adequate water, lack of adequate food, migration, disintegration of the tribes, or it could have been because the Toltecs defeated them militarily and completely eliminated them from power, but no one knows.

Jorge thinks that the leaders of the Mayans, an elite group, were stripped of their powers and taken from their high places by the workers and ordinary Indians, much like what happened in Europe when the Roman empire was destroyed by the Huns, Visigoths and others. The progress of civilization was disrupted for over a millennium as a result of the barbarian's plunder of what still is the greatest civilization the world has ever known. The Romans had indoor plumbing, hot water and other amenities which disappeared after the empire was destroyed. Those who had the knowledge were killed and those who remained could not continue the civilization.

Of interest to me is that discoveries have been recently made which might shed further light on the subject. Just five years ago a NASA satellite showed a mountain along the border between Mexico and Guatemala, in the southern portion of the Yucatan, which revealed an ancient ruin which has turned out to be possibly the largest and highest temple of all. The temple is called Mirador and it is located in the state of Kalacmul.

One aspect of the Mayan culture which we Americans have difficulty in fathoming is the human sacrificial ceremonies they engaged in. It is hard to imagine a civilized society engaging in such conduct. However, I wonder what people will think two thousand years from now about them and about us. Will people think that a baby could be born to a woman without sexual intercourse and that the man could make the blind see, the lame walk, the deaf hear, change water into wine, feed thousands of people with two fish and five loaves of bread and rise from the dead? I believe all that to be true, and I'm sure the ancient relatives believed all of the myths we now scoff at to be true.

In fact, I think they believed it with a passion much stronger than any religious zealot of today. The Mayans not only sacrificed their enemies, they also killed and sacrificed their most cherished people. Young, female virgins were put to death to appease the god of the harvest, or the god of rain, or any of the other gods. Yet the Mayans did that, and they did so with pride and glee.

It was, according to all of the history books I have read or everything I have heard, a public ceremony – one witnessed by the entire population. It was a ceremony of happiness and joy. They believed that by so doing their gods would protect them and provide for them. And they carved the hearts out of those sacrificed while the spectators watched. Most unbelievably of all, the persons sacrificed thought it was an honor to be sacrificed and willingly submitted themselves to be sacrificed.

The point is that the people of those days believed all of the myths, legends and stories with a fervor that few on this planet have. I doubt that Jorge believes that the dwarf of Uxmal was hatched from an egg by a scheming witch, but when Matthew and David Sky called him the dwarf of Uxmal, he truly was not offended and never says anything to make them stop calling him that name.

There is a cultural revolution taking place in Mexico now. People are being taught to speak Mayan. The music of the Mayan is enjoying a rebirth. The interest in their ancient temples continues to grow both inside Mexico as well as from without. Though deemed idolatry and the work of devils by the Jesuits, their ways were kept tucked away in their hearts and minds for centuries and are now being viewed with the respect accorded the Roman gods Romulus and Remus and the gods of ancient Greece. I hope that the sections of this book dealing with the Mayan civilization was both informative and of interest to readers. I think it helps explain who Jorge is.

As for the third major issue in the book, that being the Mexican culture and its relations with the U.S. over the years, the conquest of Mexico by the Spanish in the 1500s, and all that came with it, remains the dominant "footprint" on the society, including the catholic religion. Jorge is a Catholic. An overwhelmingly large percentage of Mexicans, estimated to be upwards of 90%, are Catholic. All of Jorge's ancestors were forced, at the point of a sword, to abandon their beliefs of thousands of years, in an instant, and become followers of Christ.

When the Spaniards' conquest of the Yucatan was declared to be complete in 1546, twenty five years after Hernan de Cortez' conquered the Aztecs, the Franciscans under Friar de Landa, among others, took control and became more authoritarian and powerful than the soldiers.

Conversion to Christianity was forced upon them under penalty of death. Indigenous people were required to attend mass both morning and night, pay tribute, wear shoes, live in cities, have but one wife, go to schools, learn to speak Spanish and forbidden to keep any vestiges of their prior ways, which meant giving up the religion and the gods they had worshiped for millenia. Any who continued to honor the traditions of over two millenniums were killed. They were forced to follow the teachings of the priests to the letter and the point was made so forcefully that Catholicism in Mexico remains deeply imprinted on their very souls to this day.

The Yucatan was not part of the initial "Conquest" which began in 1518 under the leadership of Cortez, who set sail from Cuba with eleven ships, five hundred men and a large number of horses to conquer the new-found land of what was then known as Mexico. Cortez and his men, with the assistance of tens of thousands of native tribes who hated their cruel rulers, conquered the Aztecs in short order, the official date being in 1521. The Yucatan was not conquered until 1546, or at least that is when the Spaniards declared victory.

The Spanish ruled Mexico until September 27, 1821, when King Ferdinand VII proclaimed that Mexico was free and independent from Spain. Mexico's "Independence Day" is officially celebrated on September 16 as that was the day in 1810 when the revolution began, just as July 4, 1776 was the day the American Revolution began, not when it ended eight years later.

The name "Mexico" comes from the Aztecs. They are said to have called themselves "Mexicas." They named their capital city "Mexico-Tenochtitlan." Some historians believe that the name "Mexico" comes from a Nahuatl word, "Metzthixihtlico," which, when broken down, means moon (metztli) and center (xictli), or center of the moon. They built a city on an island in the middle of Lake Texcoco, not far from what is now Mexico City. The following is an ancient saying about the city attributed to the Aztecs:

The place where the eagle screams,
where he spreads his wings;
the place where he feeds,
where the fish jump,
where the serpents coil up and hiss!
This shall be Mexico Tenochtitlan
and many things shall happen there.

Other historians believe the name comes from one of their gods, called "Mexitli," which was their god of war. When put together with the first theory, it could be said to mean "place where (their) god (Mexitli) lives." Jorge chooses to believe that explanation, that the word "Mexico" comes from the Aztec god, Mexitli, and it means place where god lives. In Spanish, the 'x' becomes an 'h' and it was called Mehico by them.

The entire area stretching from what is now Guatemala in the south well into the northwestern part of the U.S. was part of the Mayan empire for almost 2500 years, from approximately 1500 BC until 950 AD or thereabouts. It was then ruled by the Toltecs for a couple of centuries. In the thirteenth century it became part of the Aztec empire, which lasted until the "Conquest." There were many other tribes which exercised more localized dominion over the land during the intervals, but no others which dominated the entire region as the Mayans, Toltecs and Aztecs did.

After the Conquest, the Spaniards continued to exercise control over the entire area and spread their Catholic faith to the north, into California, Arizona, New Mexico, Colorado, Wyoming, Utah and into Oregon, and to the south throughout all of the Americas. The many Mission churches in the western part of the U.S. are evidence of that, as are the cities of Los Angeles, San Francisco, Monterrey, Santa Barbara, Santa Clara, Santa Fe, Amarillo, Santa Cruz, and countless others.

Guatemala, Honduras and Belize were all part of Mexico in 1821 when Independence was accomplished, but they all seceded from Mexico not long after. First it was Guatemala, then Belize and then Honduras. What had been the Mayan empire had given way to the rule of the Toltecs, then to the Aztecs, and then to the Spaniards. By the nineteenth century the land mass of what had been the Mayan empire had shrunk dramatically.

Incidentally and as an indicated in the book, France ruled Mexico for a few years during the 1860s. Its rule was short-lived as, with assistance from the United States, France was expelled in 1867.

Since that time, Mexico's only wars have been civil wars, the most significant of which being the one fought from 1910 to 1920 involving Pancho Villa, Emiliano Zapata and others who sought to restore the land to the people of Mexico. "Tierra y Libertad" was the war cry of the rebels. Too many foreigners, mostly from the United States, owned land and controlled businesses, like the railroads, power companies and other such things. At the beginning of the revolution, over half of the rural poor worked on Plantations owned by wealthy foreigners. The rulers, Porfirio Diaz (1876 until 1910), then Francisco Madero (1910 until 1914), who was followed in office by Venustiano Carranza, were overthrown when Carranza was assassinated on May 21, 1920. Turmoil and rumors of corruption continue to plague Mexico, and its currency has fluctuated wildly at times over the last century.

Since the turbulence of the 1920s, however, relations between the United States and Mexico have been relatively calm, despite whatever internal strife existed within Mexico. It has not spilled over into this country, until recently. There has been a high degree of cooperation between the two countries, though the United States has been the dominant player in the region and has advanced and developed far beyond its neighbor to the south. There was a time, however, in the distant past, when the roles were reversed. I found the history of the two countries to be an interesting side to the immigration issue and the history of the two countries helps to define Jorge, too, or at least I think so.

I hope this book gave you, the reader, a better understanding of the law regarding immigration, the issues surrounding the Mexicans who illegally come to the U.S. to work, and of the history of Mexico, the Mayans, the Toltecs and the Aztecs. However, this book is really about Jorge Frias. I hope you enjoyed meeting him and that you enjoyed his story, despite the fact that he was a man illegally in this country. He loves America and wants to be able to live here, as do millions upon millions of others around the globe.

The words from Emma Lazarus' poem, which are found at the base the Statue of Liberty, are no longer applicable. The United States no longer wants the "tired...the poor...the huddled masses yearning to breathe free." Nor does it want the "wretched refuse" of foreign shores. It does not want the "homeless" and the "tempest-tossed." Yet all of them, and more, many more, seek to live here.

Our country has many problems at the moment, but I think former Prime Minister Tony Blair's comments were most appropriate when asked about the growing dissatisfaction with the United States from countries all over the world. He said, "You don't find too many people trying to leave, do you?" People from every country in the world want to live here. I think the lyrics of the song America the Beautiful provide as good an explanation as any (in conjunction with the widely held belief that our streets are paved with gold) and I conclude this book with those words. They are:

America the Beautiful

Words by Katharine Lee Bates,
Melody by Samuel Ward

O beautiful for spacious skies,
For amber waves of grain,
For purple mountain majesties
Above the fruited plain!
America! America!
God shed his grace on thee
And crown thy good with brotherhood
From sea to shining sea!

O beautiful for pilgrim feet
Whose stern impassioned stress
A thoroughfare of freedom beat
Across the wilderness!
America! America!
God mend thine every flaw,
Confirm thy soul in self-control,
Thy liberty in law!

O beautiful for heroes proved
In liberating strife.
Who more than self their country loved
And mercy more than life!
America! America!
May God thy gold refine
Till all success be nobleness
And every gain divine!

O beautiful for patriot dream
That sees beyond the years
Thine alabaster cities gleam
Undimmed by human tears!

America! America!
God shed his grace on thee
And crown thy good with brotherhood
From sea to shining sea!

O beautiful for halcyon skies,
For amber waves of grain,
For purple mountain majesties
Above the enameled plain!
America! America!
God shed his grace on thee
Till souls wax fair as earth and air
And music-hearted sea!

O beautiful for pilgrims feet,
Whose stem impassioned stress
A thoroughfare for freedom beat
Across the wilderness!
America! America!
God shed his grace on thee
Till paths be wrought through
wilds of thought
By pilgrim foot and knee!

O beautiful for glory-tale
Of liberating strife
When once and twice,
for man's avail
Men lavished precious life!
America! America!
God shed his grace on thee
Till selfish gain no longer stain
The banner of the free!

O beautiful for patriot dream
That sees beyond the years
Thine alabaster cities gleam

Undimmed by human tears!
America! America!
God shed his grace on thee
Till nobler men keep once again
Thy whiter jubilee!"

I hope you enjoyed the book.

Pierce Kelley

About the Author

Pierce Kelley is a lawyer and educator turned author who received his undergraduate degree from Tulane University, New Orleans, Louisiana in 1969. He received his Doctorate of Jurisprudence (JD) from the George Washington University, Washington, D.C. in 1973. Following his admission to the Florida Bar, Pierce began his legal career as an Assistant Public Defender in Clearwater, Florida. In 1979 he moved to West Virginia and became the managing attorney of a legal services office in a rural five county area in the northeast corner of the state called the Potomac Highlands. In 1985, Pierce returned to Miami, where he was raised, and served as an Assistant Federal Public Defender for the Southern District of Florida.

Since 1986 Pierce has worked exclusively in the area of civil law, concentrating on personal injury, consumer and family law matters. He has served as lead counsel in over 100 jury trials and has successfully argued before the Supreme Court of Florida and the Supreme Court of Appeals for the State of West Virginia. He is currently an active member of the Florida Bar and an inactive member of the West Virginia Bar Association. He is admitted to practice in the United States District Courts for the Southern, Middle and Northern Districts of Florida and the United States Supreme Court, though he has yet to have an opportunity to do so. He is now a sole practitioner in Cedar Key, Florida.

Pierce began writing in 1989 when a freak accident in a softball game caused him a broken ankle. While convalescing, he wrote A Parent's Guide to Coaching Tennis, which was recognized by the United States

Tennis Association as being the perfect introduction and primer for parents of beginning players. Over a span of 50 years, Mr. Kelley was a nationally-ranked player as a junior, in the open Men's Division, and as a senior. He was also the president of the Youth Tennis Foundation of Florida from 1987 until 2007.

In 2000, Pierce authored his second book, Civil Litigation: A Case Study, while teaching paralegal students as an Adjunct Professor at St. Petersburg College in St. Petersburg, Florida. He taught at various colleges and universities as an Adjunct for over 25 years.

Pierce began writing his first novel, A Very Fine Line, in 2001. Since then seven more have followed, which are Fistfight at the L and M Saloon, A Plenary Indulgence, Bocas del Toro, Asleep at the Wheel, A Tinker's Damn!, A Foreseeable Risk, and Thousand Yard Stare, plus Pieces to the Puzzle, which is a collection of personal essays, and Kennedy Homes: An American Tragedy, which is an account of a major Fair Housing case Mr. Kelley was involved in during the years 2004 and 2007. Father, I Must Go, is a work of non-fiction.

For further biographical information, you may visit his website at www.piercekelley.com